THROUGH
THE
FIRE
TO BE ON FIRE

Marcus Rogers

ISBN 978-1-64079-687-4 (Paperback)
ISBN 978-1-64079-688-1 (Digital)

Christian Faith Publishing, Inc.
296 Chestnut Street
Meadville, PA 16335
www.christianfaithpublishing.com

Printed in the United States of America

CONTENTS

PRELUDE

My Story

"Jump. Go ahead and do it. You are never going to do anything great with your life. You will never accomplish your dreams, you will never preach, they will never accept you. Nobody loves you. If you want the pain to stop, just jump and end this misery."

I very clearly remember the voice of the enemy as I stood over a bridge in Chicago that crossed over Lake Shore Drive. As the cars sped past on the highway, I looked down in tears wondering if it would be better for me to just end my life now. I never forget I felt a hand on my neck and God speaking to me very clearly right before I was about to jump. He told me, "Son, I love you, and I have great plans for your life, trust Me. I want to use you greatly in this world." I stepped down from the bridge in tears and walked back home. The voice was so clear and powerful, and I never forgot that moment.

I didn't have the greatest childhood. I went through some rough times, and at the age of six, my mother came and got me from my school in the middle of the day and took me straight to an airport in St. Thomas with my brothers and sister. She was leaving my father because of issues in their marriage that were unacceptable. I remember getting to the airport in Chicago and not having anywhere to go. My mother had used the last amount of money she had to leave. She chose Chicago because that is where God had led her to go. She was German, and we had no family in the states whatsoever, but we had previously lived in Fort Polk, Louisiana, because my father was in the military.

I remember sitting down on a chair with my siblings and this lady coming up to my mother. She asked my mother if everything was okay and if she has a place to stay. We left the airport with her, and she took us to a women's shelter called Rainbow House. I remember lying on a bunk bed asking my mother every day when was my father coming. Eventually I realized he wasn't coming.

My mother literally started with nothing. She eventually got a job, got into school, and moved into her own apartment. It was very hard getting four kids around in the middle of the winter with no car. I remember her pushing the stroller through the snow, and I remember many days standing in the cold waiting for the CTA bus to come. I got into so many fights in school, I can't even count how many times my mother had to come to the school or buy me new glasses. I was always getting jumped in school because I refused to be bullied; because of my stature, my thrift store clothes, and my nerdy glasses, I was a prime candidate to be bullied in their eyes.

My mother ended up opening a home day care and leaving the day care she was working at. I remember her working so hard. Her hours started early in the morning and went as late as midnight. Somewhere during this process, I remember my mother deciding to homeschool us. One day we were walking as a family, and I had forgot to put on a belt. My pants kept sagging, and I kept pulling them up. My mother, in her German accent, decided that she wanted to homeschool me in that moment! She said, "Marcus, you want to be like the boys and the gangsters around here? No way, not my son! It's done. You're in homeschool!"

Just like that, my dreams of high school football and hanging with my friends went out the window. At first I was very upset, but it eventually grew on me. I ended up getting a full-time job at eleven years old with my mother's landlord. Mr. Pavlovich. He started me off with just sweeping corridors and washing windows, but eventually over the years, he taught me how to paint, do minor construction, and put me in charge of the maintenance and cleaning of all his four buildings. I worked very hard for this man for two dollars an hour, working eight-hour days. I remember taking fridges, stoves, and other heavy things up and down flights of stairs all by myself by strapping it on my back or dragging it by the straps. My self-esteem was very low, I was very shy, and my father wounds always had me looking for validation. Sometimes my boss would yell at me very harshly and ask me if I was stupid if I didn't get something right the first time. He was very hard on me, and I remember tearing down a whole apartment's drywall all by myself—wearing a mask to protect myself because the building was old. I remember working so hard during the summer months while other kids were playing. Sometimes if we finished early, I would go to the basketball courts. In the evening is when I got most of my homework done.

As the years went on, Mr. Pavlovich started paying me better and giving me greater responsibility. By the time I was seventeen, I was working for him and one of his wife's friends on the side for nine dollars an hour.

My mother and I didn't always have the greatest relationship. I was her first child, and she was very hard on me. I don't regret it, nor do I blame her. She did very well with such a difficult situation. She raised all of us by herself with no help from my father at all, not even financially. She never had any strange men around us, never did anything but be with us all the time, taking care of us and about seven other kids at one point. I remember one Christmas she bought me this Chicago Bulls warm-up suit and some Reeboks. This was a big deal because all our clothes came from the thrift store, and I was constantly being made fun of at school. I remember walking into school with the gear my mother had bought me, and my class literally went crazy, I am not exaggerating! Fact is she did the best she could with what she had, and I am forever grateful, and I wouldn't change anything about my childhood and how things went with her.

One time she was going off on me so bad, she kicked me out. I ran out the house, and I grabbed my skateboard and didn't think to grab anything else. I remember hearing the sirens of police cars thinking that my mom had called the police to come get me. I slept outside for three nights in the freezing cold. I didn't wash, didn't eat, and I just drank water in the city parks. I remember the enemy trying to make me feel like my mother didn't love me. I remember lying on the cold ground inside of a skate park, and a police officer coming up to me and asking me what I was doing out here, and I took off running. I eventually went back home, and my mother and I reconciled. I look back and laugh at it now, thinking about how I made the smart emotional decision to grab my skateboard and not a sweater or anything else.

We had our ups and downs, but the highlight of my week was always going to church on Sunday. I had some friends and the ability to socialize outside of my family and the day care kids, which was very rare. I eventually remember feeling like something just had to change in my life, and I ended up enlisting in the army. I remember the day they came to pick me up, my mother was crying. I had never seen my mother cry before, and since then, I think maybe once. I thought I was doing her a favor by joining the army. I just remember thinking to myself that it would be one less burden, one less thing she would have to worry about. I remember my brother Maurice walking me to the car and hugging me. He looked very sad as the car pulled off. Remember, my family has no family inside Chicago. It was always just us, so for me to leave, that kind of hurt my family.

I went through training and ended up being stationed at Fort Eustis, Virginia. I backslid during my first year in the military. I started partying, hitting clubs, and just acting wild. I ended up losing my virginity and opening the door to sex. I got her pregnant, and I married the girl. We went to church together, and I left all the craziness behind me. My marriage was pretty rough, and it often felt like I had just kind of picked up right were my childhood had left off with the fighting and yelling. Like I said with my mother, I don't blame my ex-wife for anything. I did not understand women, nor did I know what marriage took or what it meant to be a man, let alone a man of God. Before we had even been married a year, I was deployed to Baghdad, Iraq. This really took a toll on my marriage during that year. My daughter was born about a month after I left, a day after my birthday. I remember the long hot days standing in the sun sweating in 110- to 120-degree heat, wishing I could go home. I remember the attacks, the rockets flying into the camp, and wondering every day if I would get killed by an IED, suicide bomber, or sniper fire. I saw a lot of crazy things during my deployment. When I came home, I kind of just looked at the state completely different. I realized how unappreciative people are here. We kind of made it through the next year up and down with my marriage, and then unfortunately, I got orders to deploy again, this time to Afghanistan. This deployment was very bad for me spiritually. I backslid once again and was involved in adultery and other mess. I remember often thinking I was going to die without repenting and go to hell. When I made it back home, my marriage was pretty much over with. We tried to keep it going, but it really wasn't coming together. I continued my cheating ways and kept hitting the clubs. I was fighting all the time in the clubs and got into some very ugly situations. One night I remember getting jumped with two of my friends by over thirty people. I lay on the ground getting stomped out thinking I was going to die. I remember praying to God that if He got me out of this situation, I would go back to church and do right. Somehow I made it out of that situation alive. Eventually my wife left me, and I never chased her. I continued on in my sinful ways, and the next time I went to the club, I was involved in a shootout. I was boxed in by five cars, and I remember seeing all the guns pointing out the windows. I remember my friend in the back saying, "It's okay, we can all die tonight." He reached down under the seat of the truck and grabbed one of the pistols and slung it out the window. I remember thinking, *I can't die tonight. I am not ready to stand before Jesus.* I looked over at my best friend who was sitting in the passenger seat, and I remember just feeling like we told each other goodbye without saying it verbally. I remember one of the guys getting out of the car and walking up to the window, cocking his pistol ready to shoot me in the driver's seat.

That's when it happened. The same voice that spoke to me when I was going to kill myself when I was a child spoke to me again and said, "Look up." I remember looking up and staring into the rearview mirror. I felt my mother praying for me. It was just this feeling that I can't really explain. When I looked up in the mirror, I realized that the cars had boxed us in, in the front, but the back was wide open. I remember the guy coming closer to my window as I slapped the truck into reverse and hit the gas. Bullets started flying, and I could hear them hitting the truck. We fled down the street, and the cars followed us for a distance. We all made it home, and no one had been hit. All five of us were injury free. We examined the truck, and you could see the bullet holes in the roof and on the side. In the passenger seat door, a bullet had actually got stuck right in the frame right along where my best friend's head was.

During this time, I was shacked up with my current wife. I was making rap music and doing little shows here and there. I had met with a few secular artists and was getting a lot of support with the music. We ended up renting out a club to shoot a music video. During this whole process, I felt God just drawing me the whole time and telling me that He had something more for my life. I feel like He allowed several things to happen to kind of discourage me from continuing down the path I was headed. I remember really thinking that things were about to take off with the music, but the feeling from God was so strong. When the video was done, and my friend brought it to me, I remember watching it and feeling like a door was closing. I told him, "I can't do it, brother. I feel like God has something else in mind for me." At first he thought I was crazy, but he respected me enough to let it be. I started going back to church and my relationship with God became secure.

Everything was going great, and my wife and I got married. Once we got married, things got very hard for me once again, and I felt like I had picked up where things stopped with my last wife. I also was taking care of my brother at the time, and life was just overwhelming. I was working three jobs at one point trying to take care of all my responsibilities. I was doing the army thing and working a hotel job till midnight, and on the weekends, I was doing roofing.

It was a long process, but my relationship with God grew stronger and stronger. My marriage was going through hell the whole time though. I remember her leaving several times, and I always fought to get her back. Things were the worst they had ever been in my life outside of relationship with God. I remember oftentimes thinking I was happier when I was in the world. Why am I so miserable trying to do the right thing. I remember so many times I wanted to quit, I wanted to give up, and I thought my life just wasn't fair. I thought about my childhood and where I was now, and I would feel the bitterness trying to overtake me. I ended up getting orders to deploy to South Korea.

This was the best and worst year of my life. Through all the hell I was going through, I remained faithful. My marriage was completely destroyed. I mean all the way, done deal, pull the plug, over. I remember never being as hurt in my life as I was when I was in Korea. I would say that the fire was hottest while I was in South Korea, but for some odd reason, when I look back at it, it was the best year of my life.

In South Korea is where my purpose and my ministry really unfolded. There was a lot of temptation, a lot of hurt, and a lot of bad thoughts I had to fight off, but I remained faithful to God the whole time I was in the fire. This is where God taught me how to live in the fire. This is where God showed me He is with you in the fire. This is where God showed me there is a purpose to the fires of life we get thrown in. This is where I found out you go through the fire to be on fire, and once you get on the other side, God will do some amazing things in your life. See, before, I would always try to avoid the fire, get bitter about the fire, or complain about the fire. God has taught me to embrace the fire, and He showed me that everything I went through in this life was for a reason. I want to share with you the journey and lessons He taught me along the way that have brought me to the point where I am now and that will propel me to the place God is trying to take me.

INTRODUCTION

Don't Throw in the Towel Just Yet

As I write these words, I am living in the fire. I am not writing to you something I have not lived through. I know what it feels like to go through some very hard situations. The reason I describe it as walking through the fire is because fire can consume you, burn you, and make you sweat. You may be worried about being consumed by bills, problems, your responsibilities, insecurities, marriage problems, or even your past. When we start feeling cornered by these things in our life, we start to sweat from the heat and the fear that we will be destroyed in the fire. It is not a good feeling watching your life or the things you love going up in flames. It can be hard to stand tall as things burn around you, and not succumb to the fear in your mind.

From the place I stand, there are several individual fires in my life all around me. I tried to focus on one at a time and put them out, but they have spread and joined together to become this raging inferno of destruction. I often find myself wanting to ask God, why is this happening to me? Other times I find myself wondering how much heat does God think I can handle because this seems to be getting too hot for me to stand. I have survived many fires in my life before this one, but it is different stepping on a small fire and putting it out with your foot, as opposed to being surrounded by walls of fire all around you. It takes something more than your feet to survive this one. Sometimes God won't allow the fire to be put out no matter what you do. Sometimes God will allow the fire to completely consume everything, or burn much longer than you are comfortable with. God wants you to have faith in the fire. He does not want you to avoid the fire, run from the fire, or always try to put the fire out. He wants you to learn how to survive and live in the fire through faith. God wants you to be able to stand in the midst of the fire and not panic, but lift your hands and worship Him through it all.

This is not my first time in the fire, and it will not be my last. One thing I have learned about life is there are seasons for everything. I have had my share of good months, as well as bad. Many of the chapters you will read in this book were written during the different seasons I was going through. God showed me something amazing in every season I was in, and I started writing it all down. You can make a choice while you are in the fire. You can try to seek God, or you can give in to your emotions and feel sorry for yourself. I always tell people being a winner is a choice. You can either be a victor or a victim.

Over the last couple of weeks, it seems everything that could go wrong has gone wrong. I feel like I am in a house that is completely on fire, but I am unwilling to move. I can see the front door, and my path is clear, but a voice is telling me to stand still. Everything within me is telling me to run and never look back, but the voice tells me to stand still and embrace the fire and let God show Himself mighty. It does not feel good as the flames get closer to consuming me. I can feel the tickle of the heat against the skin of my soul, but I stand still though the flames are very threatening and spreading fast. I hear another voice telling me to run, flee, and give up. This voice often tries to suggest that God has forgotten about me or that He is not concerned with what I am going through. The voice of the enemy whispers, "Look, the flames are destroying everything, there is no hope for you. You might as well leave this spot you are standing in and do your own thing and figure things out your own way." I know the easy thing would be to give in to my flesh, my fear, and the bitterness and run, but I refuse to lose ground to the enemy no matter what it looks like around me.

THROUGH THE FIRE TO BE ON FIRE

My marriage from the outside looking in is beyond hope. We have been on the verge of breaking up for years. When I went to South Korea for a year, things were worse than ever before. Through all the disagreements and heartbreaks, I often find myself looking at my marriage in the fire thinking I should just run toward the exit sign. I have tried so hard to hold on to this marriage, but it is like holding on to hot metal, and my hands are being burnt. My flesh is saying, "Let go, it hurts," but the Spirit of God is telling me God's grace is sufficient for me, hold on and don't give up. For a few chapters in this book, my wife and I were separated, and I fell before the face of God looking for any kind of hope, strength, direction, and encouragement He could give. That is where a lot of the concepts in this book were birthed, right in the middle of the fire.

I am also facing some allegations with my jobs that are completely false. I have enough evidence to defend myself, and I am confident that God will take care of me regardless of the outcome. Because of the situation that happened at my job, they feel the need to make someone pay. Of course this is taking a toll on me, on top of the fact that demotion is possible, or even being kicked out of the military after putting twelve years in. My financial situation is looking bleak. I am not in the worst situation, but I would prefer not to get demoted. Because of this pending case and my marriage situation, I am worried about my children and how I will be able to see them and be active in their life pending a foreseeable divorce. I am not sure I will get to spend Thanksgiving or Christmas with my kids, and that hurts because they are really looking forward to it. I have had a local news station lie on me and fabricate a false story in which I can't even defend myself because of military regulations. I have coworkers who look at me, and I can see in their eyes they think that I am crazy. I have hundreds of people talking bad about me on social media, waiting on every move I make to scrutinize everything I do or say. It can be very stressful at times, and I always hear the voice of the enemy trying to suggest that I quit, give up on God, or go back to my old ways because there is no hope.

The only security I have right now is my faith. Everything around me is uncertain. Right now I am in a pending status in my life. My marriage is pending, my job status is pending, my future career is pending, and my relationship with my children is pending. What do I do in this state of unending uncertainty? It is easy to have a pity party. It is easy to feel sorry for myself and quit. It is easy to give up and run. It is easy to just throw in the towel and say, "God, this is too much for me to deal with, I give up." But God has brought me too far from being the person I used to be for me to turn back now. It does not feel good, but I refuse to drop my cross, my worship, my praise, or my faithfulness to God. I know that is what the devil is after.

I am not sure how all of this will play out. I am not sure if I will like the results. Even though I want them, I know I won't get all the answers overnight. So in the meantime, I have chosen to stand up in the middle of that fire and lift my hands up and worship God with everything I have. I worship God with tears in my eyes and with a broken heart. I worship God like I am in the most blessed season of my life. I worship God even though my mind and my flesh do not feel like it. My worship in this fire is an outward expression of the inward truth in my heart that I trust God in this fire. I am not denying that the fire is hot. I am not denying that the flames around me are intimidating. I am not denying that the closer they get, and the more I begin to sweat, the worry tries to overtake me. I am not denying that I feel fear, but I refuse to let go of my faith in God. I make the conscious decision to beat down that fear into submission every day through several tactics I will discuss in this book. I am learning how to worship, praise, be faithful, stay consistent, have faith, be productive, be a winner, survive, and fight in the fire. Everything does not have to shut down because you are in the fire.

I worship God because I have made up my mind to trust God no matter what comes. I refuse to let the heat of the flames stop my worship or steal my joy. I refuse to let the uncertainty around me make me doubt the God who stands before me and lives within me. I realize we can claim to have faith out of our mouth all day, but when it is tested, we will see where we really stand with God. Being thrown in the fire is a chance to prove how strong our faith in God really is. I trusted You when life was a beach and everything was going good, God, but that does not really prove anything. Can I trust You when I feel threatened, broken, lonely, and all hell is breaking loose in my life?

Why am I able to survive in this fire? Why has the heat not consumed me? Why is the aroma of my worship still being lifted through the smog of smoke? Is it just my personality? These thoughts have gone through people's head when they look at everything I am going through in my life, but I realize this is the greatest way to win people to God and encourage those who may feel like giving up. They see you in an impossible situation surviving, and they want to know how you are doing, so this is why I wrote this book. I want you to know that if you have a Goliath of a situation in front of you, there is a David waiting to come out inside of you.

You may be facing some difficult situations in your life right now. You may feel like you have to take matters into your own hands. You may feel like turning your back on God and just throwing in the towel. I want to encourage you to hold off on the walk of defeat.

You may be in a similar situation where it seems all hell has broken loose around you. You may see the flames threatening to consume your life, your marriage, your children, your job, your hope, your peace, and your dreams. Before you throw in the towel, I want to encourage you to read this book to the last page. I want you to know you can survive in the fire. I want you to know you can overcome what you're facing right now. I want you to know that it is not over just because it looks that way to the physical eye. There is a purpose in your pain. You may be burned, but you are not consumed. Take this journey with me, and learn how to overcome and live in the fire!

One thing I have learned about life is there are seasons for everything. Life is a series of highs and lows. Some people self-destruct during the low times of their life, but when you walk with Jesus, you learn to level out throughout the highs and lows of life. The Bible says in Ecclesiastes 3 (New Living Translation, NLT):

> For everything there is a season,
>   a time for every activity under heaven.
> A time to be born and a time to die.
>   A time to plant and a time to harvest.
> A time to kill and a time to heal.
>   A time to tear down and a time to build up.
> A time to cry and a time to laugh.
>   A time to grieve and a time to dance.
>   A time to scatter stones and a time to gather stones.
>   A time to embrace and a time to turn away.
> A time to search and a time to quit searching.
>   A time to keep and a time to throw away.
> A time to tear and a time to mend.
>   A time to be quiet and a time to speak.
> A time to love and a time to hate.
>   A time for war and a time for peace.

What do people really get for all their hard work? I have seen the burden God has placed on us all. Yet God has made everything beautiful for its own time. He has planted eternity in the human heart, but even so, people cannot see the whole scope of God's work from beginning to end. So I concluded there is nothing better than to be happy and enjoy ourselves as long as we can. And people should eat and drink and enjoy the fruits of their labor, for these are gifts from God.

CHAPTER 1

Flying and Crashing

From the moment we are born, we experience what it feels like to need. As soon as we exit the womb, we begin our search for something. There are different feelings and voids inside every one of us that are demanding to be met. Every single one of us has experienced what it feels like to need. At some point in your life, you will feel the need to be fed, held, comforted, loved, accepted, forgiven, connected, and so much more. Depending on how you grew up, who your friends are, and what your past is like, some of these needs can have a greater deficiency than others. You may not feel like you got a fair hand dealt to you in life. People often feel they got cheated out of some essential needs in life. If they didn't get what they needed as a child or in the marriage, they struggle with a void inside them. This causes many people to wander through life focusing on trying to have these needs met. The problem is many times what they use to try to fill that void only causes more damage and emptiness. The thing that they think they want is not the thing that they need at the moment. Some wounds, emotions, and needs can only be met and fixed by God. You wouldn't take a laxative for a headache, but this is what so many people are doing when they try to fix their life, and they don't even realize it. They keep trying to fix their afflictions and fill their voids with things that can't do the trick. It might make you feel high for a little bit, but the side effects will make you crash hard.

We were all born with a need. Sadly the greatest need we need to have met is never found or experienced by most people who live life. When God created men and women, He created us with a void that only He could fill. This fulfillment only comes through having a genuine relationship with Jesus. Many people spend much of their life trying to fill this void with other things and fail. They spend their whole life chasing money, relationships, sex, fame, and earthly possessions—never realizing that these things will never fill that emptiness. They are looking for the happiness, peace, or joy that they think will come with these things. They try to find peace at the bottom of a liquor bottle. They try to find love through sexual acts. Many people never come to the realization that relationship with Jesus Christ comes with all these benefits. They escape their problems while they are drunk, watching pornography, having sex, doing drugs by acquiring this momentary high. Once the high from the act is done, they realize it only made them feel food for the moment or for a few days. The effect is never a lasting one, and this is where the addiction comes into play. They keep chasing that feeling in order to escape everything else around them. What is so much better about a relationship with God is you don't have to escape your reality because He can change it. Sadly some will never ever give God a chance to show them how wonderful He really is. They continue to live lives of temporary highs going from one thing to another in a continued cycle of flying and crashing.

You may have a good season where everything is going right. You may be in a wonderful relationship, your money is in order, and your job is going great, but like everyone knows who has lived life for more than a day, these highs are temporary in life. The Bible says God rains on the just and the unjust. Eventually seasons change, reality settles in, problems will come, and you see that life is a series of ups and downs you have to face. That is why chasing these earthly highs can never fill the void or satisfy that desire inside of you. That new car will get old. That new happy relationship will have its first fight. That money will have unexpected bills. The new clothes that you just had to have will eventually be sitting in the back of your closet somewhere rarely worn. When people depend on these material things or people to be the foundation of their happiness, they crumble every single time. There is only one person you can count on to never let you down, and that is God.

> The steadfast love of the LORD never ceases;[a]
> his mercies never come to an end;
> they are new every morning;
> great is your faithfulness.
> (Lamentations 3:22–23, English Standard Version)

You can make a list of all the material things you want in life and every quality and attribute you want in a spouse, but it still would not fill the void inside you. There is nothing perfect but God. You may feel happy and experience some good days because of these things, but none of these things can give you eternal happiness. You could have all the money in the world, but yet we see rich people who turn to drugs or kill themselves because they never could fill the void. You could have the most beautiful wife or handsome husband in the world, but eventually looks will fade, and we see people cheat on the most beautiful people all the time. Eventually you get over the looks and have to live with a personality, and this personality will not always match yours. This other personality will let you down, rub you the wrong way sometimes, and just not be able to say the right things, and be everything you need every single time. This person may wake up one day in a great mood, and you may not feel the same way, so there is conflict. People are not perfect, so you can't expect perfect love from them. Perfect love can only come from a perfect God. I have always said that you should never look to a spouse to complete you. No one can complete you but God. Every other relationship should only complement what God is already doing in your life.

Imagine a young girl growing up without her father. This will create a void in her life. Many women spend their whole life trying to fill that void by chasing after men. This ends up causing more damage because many of them struggle with self-esteem, and they don't know their worth. Having a good father in their life would give them something to compare all men she encounters in life, but without having that good father figure, she is subject to trial and error. She ends up getting involved with guys who take advantage of her, impregnate her and leave, and cause emotional and even physical damage. Her marriage could even suffer because she is not looking for a husband, but looking for a father. A father loves unconditionally, and many girls who grew up without their fathers will test the limits of their husband to see if they will love them with that unconditional love. The problem is no matter how much that husband tries, he can never be her father. Yes, it is unfortunate she grew up without her father, but the only one who has the power to fill that void is Jesus Christ. The power of God is so amazing that she could turn out better off than some girls who had both parents in their homes. I want you to know that we will only end up crashing when we try to fill or fix the voids in our life with substitutes. There is only one person who can make us complete regardless of what the void is in our life. That person is Jesus Christ!

Many people waste so many years chasing these things to make them happy or expecting people to make them feel good, feel complete, or feel happy, that they become bitter or even depressed. They spends years investing in something, and they wake up and realize one day that what they invested in never fixed their problem or filled their void. Many have defined it as a midlife crisis, but I just believe that this is people who never realized their full potential in life. They woke up one day and realized they chased all the wrong things when they were younger, wasted time with all the wrong people, and they simply wish they could go back and change things hoping for a better outcome. They may not even know where exactly they went wrong. They may think, "Well, if I had just never got involved with that person," "If I had never declined that job," "If I had never left home so early," "If I had never made that one mistake," "everything would be completely different, and I would be happy."

I am here to tell you today that even if they were able to build a time machine and go back and make different choices, without a relationship with God, and having Him at the center of those choices—life would still be a series of flying and crashing. They would still wind up at the same conclusion, with maybe just a few different variables. The solution to your problem is not a different spouse, more money, bigger fame, more friends, better kids, a bigger house, better parents, or nicer possessions. The answer is a life that revolves around Jesus Christ no matter the highs or lows that come your way.

I want you to know that today is the day that your whole life can change for the good. It takes a new perspective. That new perspective can only come with a relationship with Jesus Christ. You have to put Jesus over anything and everyone else. You don't have to spend the rest of your life looking at your past full of regret. You can let the past be the past and focus on your future. Your best days are ahead of you if you start letting Jesus be the center of your life.

You have many types of relationships in your life, some are stronger than others. Some may just be a work relationship or a casual friendly relationship. Some relationships may be an "I'll only call when I need you" relationship. Some may be bad relationships or a relationship of comparison. There are different pros and cons to all these relationships, but the relationship you will benefit most from is an intimate relationship with Jesus. The closer you get to Him, the greater the blessings and benefits. We waste so much time investing our energy into relationships that do nothing for us. If you give that time and effort to Jesus Christ, I promise you will be happy with the results!

Have you ever been around someone who just made you see life, or even yourself, in a whole different way? Through a relationship with them, they opened up an entire new world of perspective that you had never seen before? This is what Jesus can do for you. Walking with Him will change the way you see life. It will change the way you look at yourself in the mirror. It will change your goals and what you think is important. It will take low self-esteem and give you confidence. It will take your wounds and give you peace. It will erase a hurtful past and give you a bright future. It will take away that worthless feeling and give you purpose. It will take away that emptiness and make you feel complete. It will take away that lost feeling and give you direction.

Think about it this way: you wouldn't just tell a random person on the street intimate or embarrassing things about your life. When you meet someone new, you test them with little bits of information about yourself over time, and as your trust builds, you begin to share more. It is the same thing with God. He wants to become your best friend. The more time you spend with Him, and the more you trust Him with the things going on in your life, the more He will reveal and share to you. When you become God's best friend, He will share secrets with you about Him and about you that you didn't even know, and when this happens, your perspective on life will change.

I like to call this Faith Glasses. You have been going through life flying and crashing and having this blurry perspective on life. You are not sure what you are supposed to do, who you are supposed to be, or who you are supposed to do it with. You have kind of just been learning through trial and error like a lab rat. You have just been going out there and testing things out. Whatever opportunity comes along, whatever guy or girl crosses your path, you just kind of deal with life in the manner of whatever falls into your lap. You might test it out and see how it goes. Well, I have some great news for you. You don't have to be a lab rat anymore. You don't have to expose yourself to things in life and just test it out and hope for the best and see if you fly or crash.

We have a Divine Creator who has a purpose for you.

> The word of the LORD came to me, saying,
> "Before I formed you in the womb I knew[a] you,
> before you were born I set you apart; I appointed
> you as a prophet to the nations." (Jeremiah 1:4)

He formed you and shaped you with great purpose. He has a plan for your life. You don't have to walk about with no direction. You don't have to leave your future up to chance. We have a God who holds it all in His hands.

In the following chapters, I will show you that with God's plan, there comes a process. I will teach you how to trust this process, put on your faith glasses, and start seeing your life in a brand-new way.

You will still have ups and downs in life, but through those ups and downs, with Jesus as your pilot, you will level out. I will show you how to look at the crashes in your life from a biblical perspective. You will realize that when Jesus is on your side, even the bad things in your life can turn into something beautiful.

If you have tried everything else, I encourage you to try Jesus. The Bible says in Psalm 34:8, "O taste and see that the LORD *is* good: blessed *is* the man *that* trusteth in Him."

CHAPTER 2

This Is No Vacation

Have you ever noticed that the more you press toward God, the more it seems the enemy attacks you? Have you ever wondered why it seems like when you started trying to live right, started trying to pray more, started trying to be more faithful to church, started trying to be a Godly spouse, a better worshipper, all hell seems to break loose in your life? Nobody ever wanted to hang out with you before, and as soon as you make up your mind to go to church on Sunday, everybody is calling your phone for you to go to the club on Friday. Maybe you decided to stay away from sexual sin or work on your marriage, and one of your exes just pops back up into your life. Maybe you couldn't ever find a babysitter before, and now with temptation afoot, someone offers out of nowhere to watch your kids for the whole night?

The devil does not bother people who are not walking down the righteous path. He is perfectly fine letting them walk to their doom, but once he sees you taking those steps toward living a righteous and Godly life, he will throw things in your way to hinder, discourage, or distract you! Understand the devil does not kick a dead horse. He has no problem with you knowing your Bible as long as you don't know the author. He has no problem with you listening to preaching as long as you don't apply it to your life. He has no problem with you getting your shout on in church, as long as you go back home and still live in a way that is contrary to the Word of God. The devil loves letting you be a casual Christian or letting you be lost in the world. Casual Christians are the first casualties! You are not a threat to him like this. But when you make up your mind that you are going to start seeking God like never before and start applying the preaching to your life and to start being a doer of the Word, not just a hearer, that is when the devil starts sweating. When you start making these kinds of moves, the devil understands that God will start making moves in your life. God will start showing you His plan for your life. God will start leading you toward the promises He has for your life. God will take you to such a deep place in relationship with Him that will completely change you.

See, the devil is not scared of those who play church and never change. He is scared of those who allow God to change them and be ruler over their life. He is worried about those who allow the transformation to take place that comes with a true relationship with God. Religion does not faze the devil, relationship with God terrifies him. You don't want to be a joke to the devil. The devil is looking at many of the "Christians" in this world and laughing hysterically. If you notice, we live in a world where everybody claims to be a Christian, but they are so blind and far from God, it is heartbreaking. The Bible mentions these kinds of people. They live their whole life thinking they are good to go, but they will be in for a rude awakening when they stand before the throne of God. The Bible says in Matthew 7:22–27 (New International Version):

> Many will say to me on that day, "Lord, Lord, did we not prophesy in your name and in your name drive out demons and in your name perform many miracles?" Then I will tell them plainly, "I never knew you. Away from me, you evildoers!"

> "Therefore everyone who hears these words of mine and puts them into practice is like a wise man who built his house on the rock. The rain came down, the streams rose, and the winds blew and beat against that house; yet it did not fall,

because it had its foundation on the rock. But everyone who hears these words of mine and does not put them into practice is like a foolish man who built his house on sand. The rain came down, the streams rose, and the winds blew and beat against that house, and it fell with a great crash."

If you're one of those Christians who never has any problems or attacks, you are a Christian who is not living up to your full potential in Jesus Christ. If you were a threat to the devil, he would do everything in his power to stop you.

When you put your life in God's hands and obediently start to surrender your ways, your heart, and your mind to Him, you enter into what I like to call the process. During this process, God begins to form you into a powerful tool to be used in His hand. You become a weapon against the kingdoms of hell. The devil does not want this for your life. He does not want you to become everything that God has called you to be.

We have an old saying in the army, "Be all you can be!" The moment you gave your life to Christ, whether you like it or not, you put on a spiritual military uniform, and you became a target for the enemy. There is a war going on between God and the devil that really has nothing to do with you.

If you look at the story of Job, the devil came to God, and they had a whole conversation about Job; and Job wasn't even there. The devil told God, if God removed His hedge from around Job, Job would turn his back on God. God allowed the devil to touch Job, just to prove a point to the devil and get some glory out of Job's life. The battle was never Job's—it was the Lord's. The Bible says in 1 Peter 4:12–14 (King James Version):

Beloved, think it not strange concerning the fiery trial which is to try you, as though some strange thing happened unto you: But rejoice, inasmuch as ye are partakers of Christ's sufferings; that, when his glory shall be revealed, ye may be glad also with exceeding joy. If ye be reproached for the name of Christ, happy are ye; for the spirit of glory and of God resteth upon you: on their part he is evil spoken of, but on your part he is glorified.

You should be happy when the enemy attacks you, in a manner of speaking. The enemy attacking you is really a sign that you are doing something right. When everything starts getting crazy and you start walking down the path of Christ, just know that is the devil trying to discourage you and get you to retreat back to where you came from. The reason he does this is because he knows God has something great for you if you just continue down the path.

A casual Christian is an ineffective Christian. The devil is not worried about casual Christians. He is not worried about Christians who are fans, but not followers of Jesus Christ. Many Christians want the label *Christian*, without the Christ; they want the benefits and blessings of Christianity without the Cross and the commitment that comes with it. Jesus suffered for us. What He went through was not pretty, but the end results were beautiful. Jesus suffered, was tested, persecuted, lied on, betrayed, had to forgive, and had to die to His flesh. If we are to be followers of Jesus, we should expect the same!

Jesus called for us to take up our cross, not our vacation packets! Every great person of God in the Bible faced some huge opposition. They all faced situations where they could choose to give in to flesh, feelings, and fear, or they could choose to press on in faith and trust God. They knew they had to deny those carnal feelings for the greater good of the cross God had given them to carry. Just like with Jesus, if we endure the cross, the end result will be well worth the trip.

Then Jesus said to his disciples, "Whoever wants to be my disciple must deny themselves and take up their cross and follow me." (Matthew 16:24, NIV)

29

To take up your cross means to fully surrender to God. It does not matter if things are good or bad. It does not matter if the preaching blesses or blisters. It does not matter what you face in life; you have a made-up mind that you are going to live for God and not drop your cross. This is what the enemy fears, and this is why he tries to discourage you when you get serious about living for God. This is why all hell will break loose in your life when you start actually living what the Bible says and changing the way you live your life. When you do this, you become an effective Christian. You cannot seek God and stay the same. You cannot read your word, fall before the face of God, soak up in His presence, and leave the same way. If you do it with a sincere heart, a transformation will take place. This transformation will give you power, and it will affect not only you, but those around you as well.

Once the transformation takes place, God will give you an assignment. Before He sends you on that assignment, He will give you Holy Ghost fire! Understand that fire is contagious, and this is what the devil is scared of. You don't have to be the loudest or the most radical to have the fire or be on fire for God. Fire is also warm. If you let the love of God shine through you, it will draw the lost from out of this cold world. Fire is contagious, and people will want what you have, and by the nature of its heat, it will attract those who are cold spiritually, mentally, and emotionally. Before the apostles started their work in the book of Acts, Jesus told them to wait in the upper room, because He was would send the comforter. This comforter is the fire we need to accomplish the mission of the gospel. The Bible says in John 14:16 (AMP):

> And I will ask the Father, and He will give you another [a]Helper (Comforter, Advocate, Intercessor—Counselor, Strengthener, Standby), to be with you forever.

We see that the Holy Spirit was sent in Acts 2 (KJV):

And when the day of Pentecost was fully come,
they were all with one accord in one place.
And suddenly there came a sound from heaven
as of a rushing mighty wind, and it filled all the
house where they were sitting.

And there appeared unto them cloven
tongues like as of fire, and it sat upon each of
them.

And they were all filled with the Holy
Ghost, and began to speak with other tongues, as
the Spirit gave them utterance.

This is how revival starts. God will put a fire in you! When you
start walking with the Lord, you will gain a love for what He loves
and a hatred for what He hates. That is what He cares about more
than anything. That is why He came down to earth and died for our
sins.

The Bible says in John 3:16 (NIV):

For God so loved the world that he gave his one
and only Son, that whoever believes in Him shall
not perish but have eternal life.

The Word of God also tells us that the heavens rejoice over just
one sinner! Souls are the heartbeat of God, and every time a soul is
saved, there is a celebration in heaven. If one soul is so valuable to
God, just imagine how God feels about a soul winner. The Bible says
in Matthew 9:37,

Then he said to his disciples, "The harvest is plentiful but the
workers are few."

When you choose to be a light unto this world for Christ,
understand that lost sheep are not going to be the only thing that is
attracted to the light. Out of the darkness, the wolves will be attracted
to your fire as well. The devil wants to keep this world in darkness.

Like we mentioned before, there is a war going on between him and God that has nothing to do with us, other than the fact we choose which side to be on. The enemy wants to use you as pawn against God to attack and defy everything God stands for.

If God wants to save your soul, the devil wants you to lose it. If God wants to set you on fire, the devil wants you to be cold. If God wants to use you mightily, the devil wants to paralyze you. If God wants to bless you, the devil wants to stress you. If God wants to fix your marriage, the devil wants to destroy it. If God promised you some things, the devil wants you to doubt it. If God wants us to be faith warriors, the devil wants us to be consumed in fear. The Bible says in 1 Peter 5:8:

> Be alert and of sober mind. Your enemy the devil prowls around like a roaring lion looking for someone to devour.

Understand that Jesus never promised the journey would be easy, but the destination will be worth it. This Christian walk will not be easy, the enemy will attack you every step of the way. You might as well have a made up mind that you will be fighting him the rest of your life. You may say, "Well, that sounds discouraging. Do I ever get a break?" The Bible says in Isaiah 40:31 (KJV):

> But they that wait upon the LORD shall renew their strength; they shall mount up with wings as eagles; they shall run, and not be weary; and they shall walk, and not faint.

Many people ask why God just doesn't destroy the devil now. Why do we have to go through all this turmoil in our lives if He could get rid of Him at any time? Well, I will discuss this in the next chapter, "Dog on a Chain."

CHAPTER 3

Dog on a Chain

A dog barking at you in a ferocious manner chained up on the other side of a fence is not so intimidating. A dog chasing you down the street barking ferociously with no chain holding it back or a fence between you and it is a cause for some concern! We feel more secure seeing that there are control measures preventing the dog from getting to us. Some people are scared of dogs by nature, but they feel more secure when they see a dog that is secured by a leash in their owner's control.

You must understand that God is always in control. The Bible says He knows the very number of hairs on your head. He knows what is best for you. He is the Creator of this universe, and He created everything in it, even the devil. The Bible says He is the Alpha and Omega, the beginning and the end. He knew everything that would ever happen before it happened in your life. From the moment He said "Let there be light," He was already mindful of you. He already knew that you would be created. He already knew that He would one day die for your sins and all your mistakes. He knew you would be in a situation that would seem impossible to you. He knew you would want to quit or give up or feel like you were not getting a fair shake. Before you had a problem, He already had the answer.

At the end of chapter 2, we posed the question, why doesn't God just destroy the devil? See, God in His infinite wisdom created the bad to showcase His good. How could we know the joy of laughter if we never knew pain? How could we know why a smile is so nice if we never had tears of sorrow? How could you know how blessed you are if you never saw someone who wasn't as blessed? The Bible says God's ways and thoughts are far beyond our understanding. Notice how God put the earth at the perfect distance from the sun so that we don't burn up, neither freeze to death. Notice how He keeps the oceans back from completely covering the earth. We may not understand how He does these things or why, but we see the results of how it works out for us. When you continue to walk with God, you see that He is in complete control of even the things we cannot understand or even like.

The devil is already defeated. There is no hope for him, his destiny is already written. He may bark and growl and scratch at you like an angry dog, but just know he is a dog on a chain. He can try to intimidate you and bark so loud you turn around and go in the opposite direction of where you were headed, but if you walk with Jesus, you must know that God has control over that dirty dog, which is the devil. The Bible says we have power over the devil through Jesus Christ!

> And these signs will accompany those who believe: In my name they will drive out demons; they will speak in new tongues. (Mark 16:17, NIV)

The devil does not even realize that he is just a pawn being played by God to get glory out of our lives. See, every time the devil attacks you, and you make it through by the power of God, the enemy gets smacked down. Every time the devil tries to throw something in your path to discourage you, but you press on in the name of Jesus, the devil gets smacked down. Every time you resist temptation in order to live a life that is pleasing in the eyes of Jesus, the devil gets smacked down. Every time you fulfill God's will for your life despite all the opposition, the devil gets smacked down. Every time a marriage is restored, a body is healed, a battle is won in the name of Jesus Christ, and the devil is smacked down.

Every time you obey the Word of God, the devil is getting smacked around. When you love your wife as Christ loves the church, even though she may not be acting the best, the devil is getting smacked down. When you respect and honor your husband and being that Proverbs 31 woman, even though your husband may not deserve it, the devil is getting smacked down. When you forgive that person who did you wrong, even though they may not deserve it, or even accept your forgiveness, the devil gets smacked down. When you love your enemy and bless those who persecute you, the devil gets smacked down.

Why is the devil getting smacked down when you do all these things? When you obey the Word of God, you are bringing glory to God, especially when you obey it through the oppositions. Like we discussed before, God will call you to forgive someone who did you wrong, but the devil will whisper justifications in your ear for you to be bitter and not forgive them. Your spouse may be acting up and could very well be under the influence of the enemy, but God is calling you to love them anyway. God will tell you to go down one path, but the devil will try to whisper from the sideline and try to get you to stray off the path and take a shortcut. If that does not work, he will try to put some obstacles along the path to discourage you and make you give up and turn the other way, but you must always remember, no matter what it looks like, God is in control. No matter what giant you face, no matter what mountain you must climb or what valley you must go through, none of it is bigger than the God you serve.

> Ye are of God, little children, and have overcome
> them: because greater is he that is in you, than he
> that is in the world. (1 John 4:4)

So when you continue to live the life of an overcomer, and you overcome everything that the devil throws your way, you are making a liar out of the devil, and God is getting the glory out of your life, and people will be attracted to this. Sometimes the things you go through in life are not about you, but it is for those around you. The biggest testimony you can ever give will not be from your mouth, but from the way you live your life. People are watching you who will never say anything to you. They watch to see how you respond to hard times and adversity. They watch you go through that hard marriage or deal with that unfair boss or face hard times financially with joy in your heart. When you respond to these trials in a victorious way—and trust God—people are going to want what you have, because we all go through things in life.

The Bible says in Matthew 5:45,

> That ye may be the children of your Father which is in heaven: for he maketh his sun to rise on the evil and on the good, and sendeth rain on the just and on the unjust.

You can worship God with your mouth, your hands, and your dance—that is fine, but the greatest worship comes from how you live your life. When all hell is breaking loose in your life, but you still trust God and press on and worship—God smiles on you. When life seems unfair, but you obey God even though it seems you are getting the short end of the stick—God smiles on you. When God told you to do something, and it didn't make sense but you followed through anyway—God smiles on you. When you fight for your marriage, you bless that enemy, you love those who don't deserve it, you forgive those who did you wrong, you refuse the enemy's temptation, you don't back down when things get hard—God smiles on you! The reason He smiles on you is because He knows you are walking by faith and not by sight, because if you were walking by sight, you would give up.

Through faith we overcome anything the enemy throws at us. Our faith is knowing that God has our back no matter what. Knowing that the devil can bark and growl, but God has him on a chain, and He is fully in control! God will let the slack off that chain just a little bit sometimes so you can just smack the devil down and let God get some glory out of your life.

Understand the devil is trying to use your life against God. The Bible says God loved the world so much He sent down His only Son to die for us. God has a deeper love for you that you could never understand. The enemy knows this and wants to use you to break the heart of God. He is so bitter and angry, he will do anything he can to try to cause God pain. You must make the choice to refuse to fear when he growls and barks, and realize that God has him on a leash.

This reminds me of my son. One day I was walking with him from the park, and a dog began to bark at him from the other side of a fence. My son got scared and started crying and ran toward me. When I picked him up in my arms, you could see that my son felt secure and safe. He turned and looked down at the dog from his new position in my arms, and he pointed his finger and said in a loud voice, "Be quiet, dog!" His confidence grew knowing he was safe in his father's arms.

You may not feel you have faith. You may panic every time something bad happens in your life. You may be wondering, how do I get faith, and how do I keep it? In the next chapter, we will talk about faith, how to acquire it, how to keep it, and how it benefits you. Remember, the Bible says,

> But without faith *it is* impossible to please *him*: for he that cometh to God must believe that he is, and *that* he is a rewarder of them that diligently seek him. (Hebrews 11:6, KJV)

In the next chapter, we will discuss what I like to call Faith Glasses and how to put them on.

CHAPTER 4

Faith Glasses

What are faith glasses? In this life, things can be uncertain. Sometimes it may feel like you are walking through life and your future is blurry, your job security is blurry, and you just can't see how you are going to make it through a certain situation. You may have experienced a failure or a letdown by someone who was close to you in these moments you may see failure or destruction, but god can turn it around and use it as a testimony. Where you have a deficiency, God can efficiently turn it around for your good.

Don't let the enemy blind you to who you are with a false perspective. All those negative voices and insecurities can be destroyed today! All those situations you face can result in victory! You don't have to live another day believing the lies of the enemy. Adam and Eve lost out on paradise because they allowed themselves to fall for the false perspective that the devil painted for them. It is time for you to check in with the spiritual eye doctor and pick up a pair of glasses that will change the way you see life.

There may be an obstacle in your life that you think you can't overcome, but when you stop looking at it through your flesh, and start looking at that obstacle with faith, you realize, "I can do all things through Christ, who gives me strength." You may be facing a giant of a problem in your life that seems so much bigger than you. You may look at it and say, "This giant is going to beat me down, this giant is going to put an end to my dreams, it's just too big for me to defeat." But when you put on your faith glasses, you look at that giant, and you realize greater is He who is in me than he that is in the world. You realize that you are more than a conqueror! Do you know what it means to be more than a conqueror? You are more than a winner, you are more than a victor, and you are a symbol of God's greatness in your life. You are a sermon of the greatness of God in the flesh. God is putting these impossible situations in front of you in order to exhibit His power in your life.

There is not a believer on the face of this planet who can navigate this life and succeed without faith glasses. The Bible says, without faith, it is impossible to please God. *Impossible* is a really strong word. The Bible also says that faith without works is dead. This means you can claim to have all the faith in the world, but if it has never been tested, then how do you really know it is alive?

This is why God allows you to go through things in life to test your faith in Him. Many people are really good at serving God with their lips, but their actions show otherwise. A true believer's character is not revealed when everything is going well, but only when all hell is breaking loose in their life. If they really believe the Word of God, and trust God like they say they do, it will show when they go through the trials and temptations of life. Many people run around and dance in church like they are victors, but have never won or fought any spiritual battles. When they are lonely, they give in to fornication. When their marriage gets tough, they get a divorce. When they get offended, they leave the church, their family, or their job. They never overcome any opposition. They praise God and sing songs about the greatness of God, but have never let it actually be put to work in their life. This is not sincere worship. Many people go to church because they just want to belong to something, or they praise and worship to be seen and accepted by people. If you can't worship God with the way you live your life and face your trials during the week, it is meaningless to try to fake it Sunday morning. Worship is not just lifting hands, dancing, or shouting, it is a lifestyle!

Many people want to give up fighting as soon as life throws one punch at them. But Paul said the race is not given to the swift but the one who endures to the end. Do you have the faith to endure, even when it looks like you might be losing the fight? Do you have the faith to trust in God that He will make a way out of no way? Do you have the faith to praise God in the middle of the storm? A true believer can praise God on the mountain as well as in the valley. A true believer can have the joy of the Lord when things are going great and when things are not so good. A true believer understands there are seasons in life, and if they hold out, God will bring them through.

Other believers want to take the fight into their own hands, and this is why they fail over and over again. The Bible says, the battle is not yours but the Lord's. When we don't have our faith glasses on, we always try to fix things on our own or try to fight our battles by ourselves. When you choose to put on your faith glasses, you realize that you don't have to panic when the enemy attacks you, because God will fight your battles. You don't have to get upset when people do you wrong, because vengeance is the Lord's. You don't have to be discouraged when bad things happen in your life, because we know that all things will work together for the good of them who love Him and who are called according to His purpose. When you have faith glasses, you can take your hands off of the steering wheel and allow God to take control. What does this mean? This means that if your spouse is acting up, you don't have to try to preach to them, make them feel bad, accuse them, worry about your needs being met, or do anything other than surrender them into the hands of a just God and pray for them. This means that when someone does you wrong, you don't have to put your hand in it and get revenge. This means that no matter what happens in your life, you never have to take anything into your own hands. You can surrender it to God and just keep on praising and pressing on until He gives you clear guidance and instructions. The greatest thing you can do with your problems is put them into the hands of God. Your problems may be too big for you to hold in your hands, but God's hand has plenty of room to spare!

You may be thinking, well, this sounds really good, where can I find a pair of these faith glasses? The Bible says, "So then faith cometh by hearing, and hearing by the word of God" (Romans 10:17).

All you have to do is get your prescription. Think of each Bible verse as your prescription. The book and verse is the corrective number on your faith lens. This means your prescription can change based on your circumstances. Knowing just one or two Bible verses or being a casual Bible reader will not be enough. The Bible gives us the keys for having a blessed life. One of those keys for success can be found in Psalm 1. This chapter talks about meditating on the Word of God and how it will make you like a tree planted by the rivers of water that will bring forth fruit in its due season. If you get rooted in the Word of God, your season will come! The problem with many Christians is they are walking by sight and what they think they should be seeing. They plant the seed of faith and then feel they can just sit back and relax until everything starts looking sunny. The fact is many believers do not recognize harvesttime because it does not look like what they thought it should look like, so they fail to reap it. Sowing is work, but so is reaping. It might not be all clear blue skies when your harvesttime comes. It may still be raining hard, but you must put on your faith glasses and still go out there and reap the blessings of God! Don't let the storm discourage you from reaping the harvest God has for you!

The more you read the Word of God, the more it will change the way you look at life, yourself, people around you, and any opposition you face. Faith will expand the horizons of your dreams, potential, and confidence. You go from thinking, *Why do I have to go through this? This is just not fair!* To thinking, *I wonder how God can get some glory out of this situation I am going through.* Or *I wonder who I will reach with my testimony when I overcome this?* The reason this happens is because you realize you cannot have a testimony without a test. You start to understand that God allows certain things to happen in your life just to see how you will respond. The more you read your Bible, the more the perspective of your faith expands. You realize that the Bible says,

But remember this—the wrong desires that come into your life aren't anything new and different. Many others have faced exactly the same problems before you. And no temptation is irresistible. You can trust God to keep the temptation from becoming so strong that you can't stand up against it, for He has promised this and will do what He says. He will show you how to escape temptation's power so that you can bear up patiently against it. (1 Corinthians 10:13, TLB)

Not everybody who claims to be a believer is a true follower of Christ. Many people follow Him only when it feels good, or it is convenient for them. As soon as the storms come or a hard trial comes along, they give up and revert back to the same old choices, lifestyles, relationships, and situations they were in. The reason this happens is because they never learn to trust God. They don't have the faith to endure and press on when things get difficult. This is why every believer must have a pair of faith glasses.

The children of Israel struggled with getting to the Promised Land for years because they always walked by sight and not by faith. In the next chapter, I want to talk to you about letting go of your idol to achieve your promise. Sometimes in order to let go of that idol, it will require some serious faith.

CHAPTER 5

My Idol or My Promise

There is a reason many people never reach their full potential in this life, and that is because they are holding on to things they need to let go of. Many people never enter into the promises of God for their life because there is no room for the promises of God in their life. Sometimes, there are some things that we need to cut off or let go of in order to be able to receive the beautiful things that God has for us. Many people often think they are waiting on God to be blessed, but the reality is God is waiting on them. He is watching you—probably shaking His head thinking, *If you would only let go of those things you are holding on to and putting before me, I could open the floodgates of blessings on your life and let it rain on you.* Too often we are holding on to relationships, jobs, people, media, bad habits, and things that we have learn to put more trust in than God. We are afraid to let go of these things even if God is compelling, and convicting us to do so, because we have more faith in these things making us happy and satisfying us than we do in God.

Some people go through their whole life holding on to their past. They never got over some old wounds. They never learned to forgive people who hurt them, or even themselves for mistakes they have made. They always look back on their glory days and just look at their future with disappointment. In order for you to grab on to your destiny, you must let go of your history. There are many people who go through life being bitter about things that happened to them in the past. They never forgive, they never overcome it, and they never let it go; and when they don't let it go, there is no room to grow. The inability to let it go and surrender it to God is a sign of a lack of faith, like we talked about in the previous chapter. If you don't have the faith to trust God with these things, you will not be able to trust God with the bigger things He has for you. God can trust us with big things, when He knows we trust Him with everything.

The reason is God knows that once He leads you to the promised land, there will be all kinds of opposition from the enemy along the way. The enemy does not want you to make it into your promised land, so he will attack you as much as he can to try to stop you, discourage you, and make you go in the opposite direction. That is why you must have faith for the battle. No matter how the attacks come, you keep going, because you know that this is just the enemy trying to hinder you from the great things that God has for you. The harder the attacks, the closer you are. The bigger the battle, the bigger the spoils.

You can look at the story of Joshua when he fought for the Promised Land. He started off fighting one king, and when he defeated that king, he gained land. Eventually two kings teamed up against him, and he defeated them and gained twice the land. There came a point where five kids tried to team up against Joshua, but he defeated them all. Understand if you defeat the small kings in your life, the enemy will start to team them up with other small kings. You may be fighting the king of lust, and then along comes the king of rage walking hand in hand. The harder you fight for God, the bigger the enemy will come against you.

You get into a fight with your spouse, and the king of rage defeats you, and you give in to it. Now that you are wounded, the king of lust slips in through your wound and poisons your mind with the options of acting on that lust. This is how we end up getting so far away from God. When you defeat one king, another one is coming, but the amazing thing is having faith and knowing that through Christ, you can defeat everything that comes your way, and no weapon formed against you shall prosper.

Victory is a choice. Being a winner is a mind-set. You can have this mind-set by getting into the Word of God. The Word of God is your sword. How can you go into battle and not have your weapon? You must take up your Bible and charge toward the Promised Land God has for you. Do not be discouraged when it seems all hell is breaking loose, and everything in the world is trying to come against you. Remember, God is in control, and just like with the story of Job, God is allowing the opposition to see how you will respond. If He sees you respond in faith and not fear, He knows He can trust you with more of the promised land for your life.

If you look at the children of Israel, they could have gone straight into the Promised Land after leaving Egypt; instead, they wandered in the wilderness for hundreds of years. They were not ready to receive the promises of God. They had not developed the character to be a good steward over the Promised Land. They struggled over and over again with putting their faith and worship in idols. What idols are you holding on to that are keeping you from entering the promised land for your life?

Your idol is anything you put in front of God. Your idol could be your social media, your spouse, your children, your fame, your sports team, or anything else that consumes your time or that you put your faith in over God. The hospital can be an idol if every time you get sick, you run to the doctor before you pray and not give God a chance to heal you. Your best friend can be your idol if every time you are going through something, you run to them and call them up before you talk to God about it. Your looks can be your idol if you put all your effort into the outside trying to catch a man or woman and have no faith that God will send you the right one for you if you just keep your eyes on Him. You can be your own idol. If you can never surrender control to God, and you feel you always need to have your hand in the mix, and always need to get revenge, debate, or prove yourself, and you never let God fight your battles, give you direction, or deal with your enemy, you are putting yourself before God.

When we hold on to our past, our feelings, our own way of thinking, our idols, and anything else—we are holding ourselves back from the promises of God. If you are full of yourself, there is no room for God in your life. Many people love calling Jesus their Savior, but they don't like calling Him Lord. You need to surrender full control of your life to Jesus. The Bible says, "Acknowledge God in all your ways, and He will direct your path." You miss out on the promised wife, the promised husband, the promised job, the promised car, the promised ministry, because you do things your own way and never acknowledge God in the moves you make. Many times people say, "I am just waiting on God," but the truth is God is waiting on them. He is waiting for them to let go and trust Him. Many times people ask why they are in a bad situation, and they want to blame the devil, but it has nothing to do with the devil. They didn't acknowledge God in their steps, so they fell into a hole. If you keep on doing that, repeatedly you will dig yourself into a pretty deep hole, and there are consequences that come with climbing out of that hole. The wonderful thing about Jesus is He is a God of mercy and grace. If we confess our sins, the Bible says, God is faithful and just to forgive us. He is not going to keep on beating you up and condemning you over and over for the mistakes you made, but you must understand that it will not be a cakewalk climbing out of the hole you fell in.

Jesus said, "Take up your cross and follow Me." Reaching the promises of God in your life will not be easy at all. The devil, your mind, and your flesh are going to fight you every step of the way. Many people never see the promised land for their life, like Moses, because they give in to one of those kings they battle with along the way. Moses was able to see it from afar off, but he never got to enter it, because he lost a battle to a king of disobedience.

Some people are bound by generational curses. Their mother was bound to drugs or was going from man to man. Their father was an alcoholic and had several divorces. Many times we grow up and find ourselves bowing to the same idols our parents did. You wake up one day thirty years old and realize you are just like your parents, your grandparents, uncles, aunts, or other siblings. I have great news for you today! You can break that generational curse. It does not matter what idol everyone else bowed to over and over again. You can crush that idol and destroy it out of your life.

Josiah was eight years old when he became king of Israel. Many of his fathers before him had worshipped idols, but Josiah made up in his mind at an early age that he would tear down all the idols in the kingdom. You can do the same! Purpose in your mind that you will not bow to the idols generations have bowed to before you. Tell yourself, "I will crush this idol in Jesus's name. I will be free today!"

If you look at the story of the three Hebrew boys, there was a lot of pressure put on them by people they lived, worked with, and worked for to bow down to the idol the king had created. They purposed in their mind that no matter what, they would not cave in to the pressure all around them, and they would stand for God. You don't have to compromise and bow to the idols of your life out of fear. You don't have to bow to the idol of lust because you feel the pressure of loneliness. You don't have to bow to the idol of drugs because you feel empty. You don't have to bow to the idol of fornication because you feel rejected. You don't have to bow to the idol of lying because you made a mistake. You don't have to bow to the idol of bitterness because someone hurt you. You can let go of those idols and have open hands able to receive the blessings and promises of God today!

What a sad thing to never be everything you are called to be and experience the wonderful things Jesus has for you because you fell to the sword of a king you had all the power to defeat. Victory is a choice, and you choose to go on or give up. You choose to live right or live in sin. You choose to trust God or to hold on to your idol, your past, or anything else hindering you from the promised land.

CHAPTER 6

The Integrity of My Loyalty

Who has your loyalty? Does your loyalty change due to circumstances that come in life? Does your loyalty change when you get around a certain group of people? Are you loyal to the Word of God only when you are around fellow believers? Who or what gets most of your time? These are important questions every believer needs to look in the mirror and ask themselves. You will never make progress in God if you are in too much denial to look in the mirror and be honest with yourself and take those character flaws and mistakes before the Lord. Many people are so loyal to keeping up a false appearance that their lies become their reality. They make choices every day based on a false reality, and this is why they never experience the blessings of God in their life. The devil will literally make a fool out of you if you allow yourself to make emotional- and carnal-based choices all the time.

Every day of this life, you will have to make choices, and the choice you make is usually based on where your loyalty lies. If you have to choose between sin and doing right, you are going to choose sin if you are being loyal to your carnal desires, and you will choose to do right if your loyalty is in God. Where you choose to place your loyalty will affect you receiving and operating in your promise. The Bible talks a lot about your spirit fighting your flesh. I like to look at it as if you only had one can of food, and you had to feed it to either your flesh or your spirit. You can only feed one and starve the other. If you tend to always choose to feed the flesh, your spirit man is going to eventually die and become nonexistent. If you never feed your spirit man, you can always expect yourself to make choices based out of loyalty to the flesh. The way you feed your flesh is your time and effort. Do you feed yourself movies, Internet, and eat junk food often? Do you have sex before marriage, entertain lustful thinking, be angry, unforgiving, have a pity party, or seek revenge? If you always show loyalty to doing what your flesh wants, and rejecting the Spirit, be assured you will never see the promised land God has for your life. In order to get to the promised land, you must walk through the wilderness. So many people enter the wilderness and quit. They turn around and go backward. They try to find some way to go around the wilderness and still reach the promised land. This will never work. You must embrace the wilderness and remain loyal to the direction of the Spirit. When you have time, feed your spirit man with Bible reading, fasting, worship, praise, and much prayer. This will give you the strength you need to endure the journey of the wilderness and make it to the entrance of the promised land. You have to choose whether you will be loyal to your flesh or to your spirit man.

If God promised to bless your marriage, you cannot be loyal to the single girlfriends who give you bad advice on how to deal with your marriage. You lose out on the promise of God by heeding the bad counsel of people. Your loyalty to those people causes you to consider what they have to say. That loyalty will cause you to feel a sense of guilt or shame for not heeding their advice or at least hearing them out. Their advice can even sound good, but just because it worked for them, does not mean it will work for you. Maybe God has a different direction for you, but you wouldn't know that if you are always loyal to running to your friends and everyone else but God when you need direction. Psalm 1 tells us, "Blessed is the man that does not walk in the council of the ungodly, or sit in the seat of scorners." This means if you want to be blessed, you can't take counsel from just anybody, and you can't hang around bitter people. Many people in your life will give you bad advice because of the bitterness in their heart. Misery loves company, and sometimes people are unable to give sound advice based off of them being blinded by hurts, bad teaching, or past life experiences. Sometimes you just have to cut ties to people and connect to God. It may only be for a season, but you may need that season of separation to achieve the direction and promises of God.

Peter had good intentions when he drew his sword and caught off the ear of the guys who came to seize Jesus. Even though his intentions were good, they did not line up with the plan and destiny for Jesus's life. Jesus told Peter to put away his sword. Judas on the other hand embraced Jesus with a kiss. Even though Judas was betraying Jesus, his actions at the time lined up with the Father's will for Jesus's life. Jesus's loyalty was to the will of His Father. He could have given in to those feelings we saw as He prayed in the garden. He asked for the cup to pass, and He could have ran and let Peter and the disciples fight off the guards or even commanded angels to come down and smite them, but His loyalty was to the will of His Father, even though the current outlook of the situation was a grim sight. The path to the cross was not pretty, but the end result of Jesus's loyalty to the process was beautiful. Because of His loyalty, we received the promise of salvation!

This world will put pressure on you to accept certain things or do certain things that compromise what the Word of God has called you to do. If you cave in to that pressure, and abandon your loyalty to the Word of God, you cannot receive the promises of God. The Bible says, without faith, it is impossible to please God. When people lack faith, they compromise their loyalty to God. If you really trust God in your heart, you will never compromise. If you know in your heart that God will take care of you, you can stand, and not worry about your physical, emotional, financial, or any other need being met. Many times people cave in to the pressure because they are depending on people or things to provide a feeling of acceptance, love, or something else to do with their overall livelihood or position in life.

Many times God will test your loyalty by putting you in hard situations. You will be faced with a lion's den like Daniel, or a fiery pit like the three Hebrew boys. You will watch people around you bow to the pressure out of fear, lust, loyalty to the wrong things, and a lack of faith. If you take a stand for God, stay loyal, and trust His Word no matter what you face, God will bless you beyond your wildest imagination.

Job lost everything but his loyalty to God. He could have been loyal to his feelings and cursed God. He could have been loyal to his wife and caved in to the pressure of her words, but he chose to keep his loyalty to God and take a stand on God's word. Because of this, God blessed him in a wonderful way. Because of Job's loyalty, even when he didn't feel like being loyal, God restored everything the enemy had stolen, and then some. Are you willing to keep the integrity of your loyalty in order to achieve the blessing?

When you are loyal to the Word of God, you will be obedient to what it asks of you—even when you don't feel like obeying. The Word of God will call for you to forgive an enemy, or bless someone who has hurt you, or let go of something you don't want to let go of. Many times God will allow you to be in a situation just to see if you will remain loyal. He will let someone hurt you, just to see if you are going to be loyal to your feelings or be loyal to the guidance of the Spirit and to the Word of God. If God puts you through the fire and you always choose your flesh—your feelings, your sin, and your way—over what the Word says, God can't give you ownership of your promise. The only reason God allows you to be tested is to see if your loyalty will not be shaken. In order for your loyalty not to be shaken, your choices must be rooted in faith.

Samson was blessed with amazing strength. The only thing he had to do was not cut his hair. That was the covenant that was made with God when he was born. His loyalty was to God, but when he fell into his lust with Delilah, he betrayed that loyalty to God and told Delilah his secret. She cut his hair, and he lost all his strength. Because of his failure to be loyal to God, it caused him much pain. The Philistines came and put out both his eyes, locked him in prison, and made fun of him and mocked God. Being disloyal can cost you!

The enemy is not going to just let you have the promised land and leave you alone. God knows this. God knows that the enemy will do everything in his power to kill, steal, and destroy the promise and blessings God gives you. God needs to see that you are loyal enough to Him to be a good steward of the promised land He gives you and places in your care. He wants to know you will protect the fire, the marriage, the anointing, the children, the ministry, the finances, or anything else He gives you.

Think of it as if God has placed a garden in your care. A garden is hard work. You have to pull weeds, water it, maybe cut grass, protect it from critters, fertilize the ground, and make sure the plants are getting the proper sunlight and so much more. Your promise is like a garden. Will you be a good gardener, or will you let the enemy come in and trample the flowers, steal the seeds, and destroy the beautiful promise of God in your life?

God needs to know this (even though He already knows what you will do way before you do it), and that is why He will put you in situations to test the integrity of your loyalty. If you choose obedience to the Word of God over your fleshly desires in every situation, I promise God will bless you in ways you could never imagine.

God will test the loyalty of your heart before He gives you the promise of your future.

CHAPTER 7

Learn the Lesson, Get the Blessing

Your pain is not in vain. We mentioned before that the Bible is clear that all things will work together for our good. It also tells us not to be surprised when we go through trials in this life. One of the things that has helped me trust God is knowing He is in full control. I know Jesus loves me, and I refuse to doubt that love for me. Because I know He loves me, I know if He is allowing certain things to go on in my life, there must be some purpose behind it that will help me. Trust and believe in Him although it may not always feel good. There have been many times I wanted to complain to God, or I felt like what had happened to me was not fair. I have been backstabbed and had my heart broken so many times, I can't even count, but one thing I have noticed as the years have went by, I have survived. As long as I have held on to Jesus and kept pressing, I have survived, and He has blessed me in a great way. Once you realize that walking with Jesus is not always a party, and that trials, hurts, wounds, tribulations, persecutions, and so much more will come with the territory, you learn to walk with a new purpose.

When I was younger, I would get hit by life and go crawl in a corner, ball up, and have a pity party. I would complain because my situation didn't seem fair, or I simply didn't like it. Many times I found myself trying to sleep away or run from my problems. One of my biggest weaknesses was women. I always ran into the arms of a woman to let her comfort me, encourage me, and love me. Every single time I did this, I got my heart broken in the long run. It reminds me of Samson. He lay in the arms of the wrong woman and paid the price. I could have avoided so much pain in my life if I had just ran into the arms of Jesus. I had to learn the hard way that no woman or anything else could help me, heal me, and love me like Jesus could. As I have walked with God and seen Him deliver me over and over again, I no longer climb into the fetal position when life hits me. I no longer end up in the bed of fornication or adultery. As soon as I feel the impact of the blow, I start looking for the lesson. Sometimes I have got hit so hard, it felt like my soul took a knee. This will happen to everyone who walks with God at some point. You will have a choice to make. You can sit there and say, "Wow, that hurt! I give up." You can sit there and say, "God, that is not fair, why did you let that happen to me?" Or you can be bitter and try to fix the problem yourself. But the best thing you can do is, when you're down on that knee, look down at the devil and say, "I will not be discouraged or defeated, and I know that this is going to work out for my good." Let the devil know that you have a made up your mind to serve God and fight back. Lift up your head and tell God, "Yes, this wound did hurt. Yes, it does seem like more pain than I can handle. Yes, it feels very unfair right now, but I trust You." Let the Lord know that you acknowledge He is in control. Ask God to show you what He is trying to teach you through this pain you are experiencing in your life.

I used to focus on the pain, and now I focus on the process. I spent years dealing with the same pain over and over again because I never learned the lesson God was trying to show me. It is not always easy to trust God when you actually feel the wound. We all have certain emotions and feelings that activate in those kinds of situations, but you must push past those things with prayer, worship, fasting, and constant Bible reading. If we don't do those things, we would lose our mind and become superdepressed. The only way we are able to endure is by constant meditation on the goodness and love of God. You have to remind yourself that Jesus loves you. The Bible says, He won't allow you to be tempted with more than you can bear.

You may think the burden is too heavy, and you want to drop it, but if God has put it on your shoulders, that means you can handle it.

I found out quick that you cannot get in God's presence and just feel the same. It is literally impossible to break through in prayer and worship and leave God's presence the same way you came in. Many times the heat of the fire makes people run to God harder than they did before. God knows exactly what temperature He needs to crank the spiritual thermostat to, to get your attention. When you give God your full attention, He can show you why you are going through what you are going through and teach you a new way of living.

Many times you are going through that fire to learn something about yourself, about people around you, and about God. When you stop focusing on the pain and start focusing on the process, you will learn the lesson faster. The quicker you learn the lesson, the faster you get the blessing.

I always tell people if you fail the test, you will have to go through it again. You can't fail your test and graduate to the next level in Jesus. There is a reason you are going through that test. I remember one of my biggest tests was keeping my mouth shut in certain situations and just letting God fight my battles. Every time I opened my mouth to defend myself, or argue, the situation would get worse. Things would calm down, but then weeks later, I would find myself going through the same exact test. Once I started learning to keep my mouth closed and let God fight the battles, the fight would end sooner, and there would be peace. I prolonged the coming of peace and resolution by trying to fight my own way through the battle.

This can be applied to anything. Have you wondered why you're still single? You keep dipping into fornication and showing God that you are not ready, nor do you trust Him to send you a spouse. Do you ever wonder why your kids keep acting up no matter what you do? You complain about it more than you pray about it, and it is time for you to just cut back and surrender them to God. Do you wonder why you and your spouse keep ending up in the same cycle? Stop trying to fix each other, and turn over the controls to God.

Many times the lesson is to show us an area we need to improve on, like me not always being so quick to speak my mind. Other times God is trying to show us how to trust Him in certain situations. He can also be trying to reveal to us certain individuals we need to remove from our lives.

If you choose on your own to be humble and embrace the correction, rebuke, and lesson, you will receive the blessing of God in your life a lot quicker than someone whom God has to break down and humble in order to receive what He is trying to teach.

CHAPTER 8

The Negativity Vaccine

This world can be a very negative place. There is so much chaos going on with the politics of this world. Every time you turn on the news, you can be sure that you are about to receive a dose of negativity. There is threat of wars all over their world, and there is so much division and hatred here in America. This negativity is constantly presented to us and trying to invade our system like a sickness.

Not only do you have to deal with the negativity going on in the world, many times you will face and be exposed to negative energy all around you. If things were not already going bad enough in your life, there are always people who love to pile on to the burden you are already carrying.

Isn't it frustrating when you are going through a hard time, and people close to you only add on to the drama? You are looking for comfort in your situation, but receive comments like "I told you so," "Well, that's what you deserve," "If you had just listened to me in the first place," "You must have done something wrong to be in the place you are." Does this remind you of any story in the Bible?

Look at the story of Job once again. God allowed Satan to touch Job simply to prove a point to the enemy. God was not allowing these things to happen to Job because he was a bad person or because he deserved the pain he was receiving. Job's "friends" came along and began to accuse Job of wrongdoing. They started offering solutions and answers that only would make a person feel worse in the current condition. Job's wife was no help either. She told Job, "Hey, you're so miserable, why don't you just give up, curse God, and die?"

Do you have people like that in your life? Do you have people telling you to give up on your dreams, your calling, your family, because it looks hopeless to them? Do you have people hating on you because you're in a season of blessing, but instead of you getting to enjoy the blessing, you find yourself defending it to people who feel you don't deserve it?

I want you to understand something that changed the way I live my life. No matter what you do, there will always be people who have something negative to say. There will always be an enemy that comes against you. You can sit there and let that negativity infect you and cause you to be depressed, give up, or be sick with bitterness, or you can press on through it. Once I realized that I could never please everybody, it was like a burden was lifted off me. I realized that I was wasting my time trying to prove myself or show my credentials to every person who came against me.

You only have one life to live, and you have to be careful what you invest your energy into. You can sit there all day trying to prove yourself to people, or you can take your time and work on improving yourself. God has put a fire inside you. You have dreams, goals, desires, and things you want to accomplish; but do you have the focus it takes to achieve those things?

You need to do everything you can to protect the fire God gave you and to build on it. The wolves will come and try to put it out and discourage you. You can sit there and argue and fight with the wolves, or you can focus on gathering wood, building your fire, and letting God take care of the wolves and fight your battles.

You look at the story of Paul when he was shipwrecked on the island, and you see a perfect example of this. When Paul came on to the land, there was a fire built for him. Paul could have just sat there, been lazy, and said, "Hey, I am going to enjoy this heat for the moment." But he chose to invest in his future and find some more wood. The Bible says, when he gathered the wood, a viper came out and bit him.

Understand that the more God blesses you and you build in this life, the more haters, negativity, and attacks you will have come your way. The more wood you gather, the bigger the fire will be, but it will also come with a few snakes! When the people saw the snake latch on to Paul, they waited for him to die. There are people watching you, waiting for you to die. They are waiting for you to give up on your dream, and on your marriage, and whatever else God has for you. The situation could look bad from the outside. It could even look worse to you from the inside, but understand dying is a choice in this case.

Things in life may have jumped out and bit you to try to stop your progress, but you must make the choice to press on. You cannot let the venom of bitter, jealous people slow you down or kill your dream. When these attacks come, rejoice because you know you are on the right path! The best thing you can do when the enemy attacks is inject yourself with the negative vaccination to counterattack the venom of doubt and negativity.

I know you are wondering where you can find this wonderful vaccination. If you search for it, you will find it in the presence of God. Well, how do I get there, you may be asking. Praise and worship is how you inject yourself with this cure! Every time you see negative things on the news, in your path, or in your life, just lift your hands and enter into the presence of God. You may have been bitten, and feeling the effects of the venom, but you must overcome that feeling to just lie by the fire and let it die out. You must overcome that feeling to just let death take your dream, your motivation, and your joy for the things of God. You must talk to yourself and say, "Lord, I don't feel so great right now, but I worship You anyways," "I don't feel like my dream is coming along like I thought, but I know You are still good," "I got all these people coming against me, and it seems I have no support, but I know that I am in Your hands," "I feel bitter, I feel discouraged, I feel betrayed, but, Lord, I cast my cares unto You!"

Something amazing happens when you can worship God despite the negative outlook of your circumstances. Something amazing happens when you have a made up mind like Job, and your able to say, though He slay me I will trust Him. Something amazing happens when people see the viper fastened to your arm, and they are wait-ing for you to die, but you don't let the snake stop your praise, your worship, your faithfulness, or steal your joy! If the viper is attacking you, it is because you are so close to reaching another level in Jesus.

Don't be discouraged to build your fire because a few snakes jumped out when you were collecting the wood. You keep on gath-ering the wood, and every time a snake jumps out and bites you, you shake it off in the fire. You don't have to run in the opposite direc-tion of the fire, you don't have to try to avoid the fire, you drag that negativity, and that enemy, and that hater through the fire with you.

Just like with the story of the Hebrew boys, the strong men who bound them and threw them in the fire were consumed. What the enemy uses to try to destroy you will be the very thing that destroys him. It won't always feel good, but if you keep on gathering up the wood, the fire that you build will be big enough for the world to see the goodness of God in your life. This world will try to inject you with the poison of fear, doubt, and negativity every day, but just keep injecting yourself with the vaccination of praise and worship, and you will make it through!

CHAPTER 9

❖————✤✤✤————❖

Your Breaking Season

Hebrews 11 is one of the most amazing chapters in the Bible. Many people have called it the hall of faith! You have an amazing layout of several heroes in the Bible who had their faith tested. You will find one commonality among them all. Every single person mentioned was at a breaking point. God had either promised them something or instructed them to do something that just seemed unbelievable. God told Abraham that Sarah would have a child, but she was past child-bearing age. As the story goes, they conceived a child, but God then later asked Abraham to take that child and sacrifice him. There are many things that we can learn from this story.

Abraham didn't just stand on faith after God gave him the promise of a child; he gave in to the pressure from his wife, and he slept with their handmaid and bore a child named Ishmael. This was not an act of faith. This was Abraham acting out of desperation in his breaking point and doing things his own way. As a result, this caused turmoil in Abraham's life. His wife and the handmaiden kept getting into it because of Sarah's jealousy. We later see that Sarah eventually gave birth to a child whom they named Isaac.

The first thing we learn here is that we have to be careful what kind of choices we make when we get in our breaking season. You may be waiting on the promises of God in your life, and it feels like you have been waiting forever. The worst thing you can do is try to act off your own intellect. The Bible says, God's ways are not our ways, and His thoughts are not our thoughts. Many times while waiting for the promises of God, we prolong its coming by messing up, giving up, and doing our own thing. When we don't trust God in these seasons, we tend to make a bigger mess of things. Sometimes God will allow us to wallow around in our mess for a while. He is waiting for us to realize that without His direction and input, we will continue to make a mess of things! Once we learn this, He is faithful to deliver us and clean us up.

Make no doubt about it, there will come a season of breaking in your life. God may ask you to forgive some people or put up with some people who are doing you wrong. He may tell you to do something you don't feel like doing or endure a situation you just want to get out of. God might put you in a situation like Job, where everything that could go wrong in your life is going wrong, and He just watches to see how you respond. God may put you in a situation like Joseph where He gave you a dream, but then threw you in a pit in total darkness and said, "Trust Me." God is going to put you in some situations where the pressure is going to be on. He will bend you, and maybe even break you, just to see what you choose to do. You can choose to trust God and say, "Lord, I know You have broken me in order to put me back together better than ever." Or you can say, "You know what, God, this is too hard. I don't want anything to do with this walk anymore. I am just going to find my own way and my own solution."

When Jesus was in the wilderness, the devil came and tempted Him. He told Him to turn the stones into bread in order to satisfy His hunger from being in the wilderness. Jesus was at a breaking point. He had a choice to make. You may be hungry for some things in your life. We all have desires, and these desires—many times—are normal, but we have to make sure that we fulfill them in God's timing.

You may be starving for a relationship, some attention, a baby, a promotion, a ministry, affection, sexual desires, forgiveness, support, love, and so many other things in this life. It is not a sin to want these things, but it can take a sin to get them if you do it the wrong way. Trying to fulfill legitimate needs in an illegitimate way can cost you big-time. The pressure from the desire to get these things can push you to a breaking point. A situation you are in where these needs are not being met can push you to a breaking point and find you looking for a sin, substitute, or shortcut to have these needs fulfilled. You have a choice to make. You must choose to wait it out in the wilderness and trust God, or go ahead and turn stones into bread and compromise for temporary satisfaction.

Esau was at a breaking point after being out hunting all day. He was hungry and ready to eat. His brother Jacob had been cooking up a stew, and the aroma hit the nostrils of Esau and probably caused his stomach to growl. When Esau headed toward the location of the aroma, his brother gave him a proposition. Jacob said, "Trade me your birthright, and I will give you something to eat." Are you willing to trade away your birthright for a moment of temporary happiness? Are you willing to throw away the promises of God because you are hungry now but don't have the patience to wait for God to satisfy that hunger?

We live in a generation where people have very low tolerance for the breaking season. They scramble and panic, and they want to get out of the situation right now. They want to stop feeling lonely right now. They want to feel appreciated right now. They want to be married right now. They want to have sex right now. They want the money right now. Because of a lack of faith and patience, they do like Esau and Abraham, and they try to make their own way. The Bible says this is like building your house on the sand. As soon as the storm comes into your life, your house is going to get blown over, and while everything is flying around, you may take on some serious damage and debt. You can invest years in a chaotic marriage only to see it end in divorce, child support, a broken home, and kids growing up without one of the parents in their life on a consistent basis. You can end up like Hagii, the handmaiden, running around in the wilderness with her son.

How we respond in the breaking seasons in our life usually determines the next couple of years of our lives. If we learn to respond in the correct way, God has no problem with keeping His word and blessing us. If we get impatient and do our own things, and bow down to the idols in our life—like the children of Israel, we may find ourselves wandering around in the wilderness for the rest of our lives and never coming into the promises of God. Is that sin in your life, that compromise really worth missing out on your birthright? Is that sexual relationship so good, that it is worth missing out on the husband or wife God has for you? Are you so dependent on that promotion that you feel the need to lie or put your family in the back burner in order to get it? Are you so selfish that you always have to have your way and have everything on your timing? How you respond in your breaking season will determine how far you go in God.

There is a reason for the season. When we go through the breaking season, God will show us how to trust Him, despite all odds we face. In order to have a miracle, you must have a problem or an impossible situation first. Once we see God accomplish the impossible in our lives, our faith hits a new level. This is so necessary because when the enemy starts to attack us, we will be unshaken because of our faith. The enemy can throw whatever he wants at you, but in the back of your mind, you will remember when God did the impossible in your life. Never forget your breaking season. Anytime the devil tries to make you feel like you are done, and defeated, remember your breaking season and what God did for you.

CHAPTER 10

These Voices Are Confusing Me

One thing you must pray to God for is discernment. I am not trying to be funny, but there are many voices you can hear in your mind. You have your own voice, the voice of the enemy, and the voice of God. You may wonder, well, how do I know which one is which? How do I know which one I should listen to and follow?

Anytime you hear any voices in your head, you must balance them off the Bible. Is what the voice telling you to do match up with the Word of God? God cannot contradict Himself. He will not tell you to do something that contradicts His Word. Many times what God is asking you to do will be at conflict with your flesh. You will have this gut feeling in your spirit to obey the voice, but your flesh will try to talk you out of it. God may ask you to forgive someone who has hurt you badly, and before you get the chance to do so, the other voice in your head is telling you they don't deserve your forgiveness, and if you forgive them, you lose, and you need to make them pay! And they need to know that they hurt you.

The way you are able to know that the voice of God is telling you to forgive is when the voice lines up with scripture. Jesus commands us to forgive our enemies and those who do us wrong. You can never go wrong when you follow the Word of God.

The other two voices you hear usually work hand in hand. The enemy will appeal to your flesh, your pride, your lust, your emotions, and give you suggestions that contradict God's will for your life. Your voice will be telling you they did you wrong and it still hurts. The enemy will jump in on that thought and say, "Yeah, you're right, it does hurt, you shouldn't forgive them," "You need to let them know they hurt you," "You need to go ahead and throw a pity party."

These voices contradict having faith in God and scripture. The Bible says, the battle is not yours, but the Lord's. When you feel like you have to make somebody pay, you are saying you don't trust God to deal with them or turn around your situation. You have become your own idol! You cannot be pleasing in God's eyes and not be trusting Him with your life. Any voice that calls on you to do things that shows a lack of faith in God—is not from God.

On the other hand, any voice that is calling you to walk by faith and not by sight is usually from God. Always pray about it before you move, and see if it lines up with scripture. You want to make sure that the voice you follow is the voice of the Spirit, and not your feelings. I learned the hard way that some people have big hearts and good intentions, but it does not always line up with the Word of God and can cause some serious trouble.

For instance, just because you know you should forgive somebody doesn't mean you have to let them back into your life. I often tell people forgiveness does not always mean reentry. You don't have to give someone full access back into your life because you forgave them. It could be your own voice telling you to give them a second chance, and not God. People who follow their heart often wind up in a cycle of abuse, disappointment, and heartache. It is always best to follow the leading of the Spirit over everything else. Your heart can deceive you or lead you down a destructive path even though it has good intentions.

Eventually somewhere during the cycle, or down the road, you look up to God and say, "Why do I keep getting stuck in this hurtful place? Why does this person keep doing me wrong?" God will let you know, "I instructed you to forgive, I never told you to allow them back into your life. You made that choice."

Many times we can also hear voices from people in our life. Maybe your parents or a teacher told you that you were stupid. Every time you try to take a test or do something that requires intellect, you hear this voice inside your head making you doubt yourself and feel that you're not good enough. Maybe you've experienced some things as a child that seemed normal to you, and when you've gotten older, you can't seem to break free from what you've experienced. You are not able to have a good marriage, or good relationships, because there is a voice in your head reminding you that this is not the way it is supposed to be. What you experienced as a child may be completely wrong, but because it was your normal, it's hard to overcome that voice you hear in the present. Maybe, often, you end up sabotaging a good thing or running away from something that is perfectly normal out of fear. Maybe your father was a cheater, and every time things get serious with a girl, you back out and panic, because you hear that voice in your head telling you are just like your father, or there is no point settling down and getting married because eventually you will cheat on her.

You have to take these things to God in prayer. I also suggest taking them to a prayer partner and a pastor you can trust. The Bible says in Proverbs 14:11, "Where no counsel *is*, the people fall: but in the multitude of counselors *there is* safety."

Sometimes we can be biased to the voices we hear, and it blocks us from getting the direction and revelation we need. It causes there to be confusion because our feelings, our emotions, our desires, and the enemy's tactics are all thrown together, and these create chaos when you do not know how to allow the Spirit to flush these things out. James 1:8 states, "A double minded man *is* unstable in all his ways."

You will never make any progress having a double mind. You need to learn to identify which voice is yours, which voice is from the enemy, and which voice is coming from God! You may feel overwhelmed and feel like your mind is getting attacked with so many negative thoughts and emotions, but there is an answer!

The Bible says in 2 Corinthians 10:5 (NIV):

> We demolish arguments and every pretension that sets itself up against the knowledge of God,

and we take captive every thought to make it obedient to Christ.

Whatever voices you hear in your mind, you must make sure they line up with what you know about God, what you know about His Word, and if you are not sure, you must have the patience to seek God. Many people give up way too fast, and they make no effort into actually seeking God for discernment, clarity, or an answer from God. They get lazy and just give in to their flesh. They continue doing this until they get into such a mess; they have no choice but to get desperate to seek the face of God! If you can't find your answer in prayer, fasting, or the Word, go seek counsel with your elders.

Lastly, I will say be very careful about who you seek counsel with. Some people are signal boosters, and others are signal blockers. Many times people refuse to be honest with themselves. They run to the person who they know is going to tell them what they want to hear, as opposed to running to the person who may tell them some truth that they don't want to receive. This is actually a reflection of your love for God being manifested through your actions.

The Bible says in Proverbs 12:15 (King James Bible): "The way of a fool *is* right in his own eyes: but he that hearkeneth unto counsel *is* wise."

If being right with God is more important to you than anything else, you will not run from counsel, you will not run from scripture, and you will do whatever it takes to make sure your steps are ordered by the Lord!

I mentioned before about people being signal blockers or signal boosters. Signal blockers will tell you what you want to hear or feed you with negativity, and this causes the signal that God is trying to send you to be blocked. Many people have their hearts hardened by pride and bitterness. People who feed into those things, and what your flesh wants to do, are really blocking the signal of God from getting through. You want to be around signal boosters. You want to seek God for a word and then get around people who are going to reinforce what you know is right and make you feel strong enough to overcome what your flesh, your doubts, your fears, your insecurities, and what any other voice is telling you. They boost the signal of righteousness and obedience unto God in your life. They help you get closer to the will of God for your life, as opposed to the will of you for your life.

It will never be easy fighting off the voices that are telling you what you want, but if you trust God and follow the Spirit, it will pay off in the long run. When you get closer to the promises of God, the devil will try to do anything he can to confuse you and make you unsure of your next step. You will have inward voices and outward voices trying to cause you to become spiritually paralyzed. The devil wants you to just stop moving. He wants you to give up on pressing forward. He wants to deceive you into believing he has a shortcut for you that will result in the same thing that God had for you—or maybe even something better. You cannot fall for this deception. The Bible says in 2 Corinthians 2:11 (NKJV):

> Lest Satan should take advantage of us; for we are
> not ignorant of his devices.

You need to be aware of the enemy's attacks to deceive and destroy you. You need to put on the full armor of God and guard yourself at all times. The devil is not sleeping or taking breaks. He is always looking for a way to destroy you. The most effective way for the enemy to destroy us is through our mind. If he can take away your joy, your peace, and your faith, he knows that it will be easy to hinder you and eventually destroy you. The devil is going to always try to attack what you know about God. If you know that the Bible says God will provide, protect, restore, forgive, and redeem you, the enemy is going to try to challenge your belief on that and make you doubt it every step of the way.

Always remember to seek out the voice of God, and follow the leading of the Spirit over and before anything or anyone else. This is how you walk into blessings and live a victorious life. No matter what voice you hear, make sure it lines up with the Word of God!

CHAPTER 11

How Do I Survive the Fire?

If you put into action all the different chapters of this book, you will have a basic blueprint for how to survive the fire and make it into the promised land. You have to understand that even though the Word of God gives everyone a general outline for success, you are still a unique individual on your own unique walk with God. The variable in your life will be different than the ones in mine, but if you apply the same basic principles, the end result will be the same. The Bible says in Philippians 2:12,

> Wherefore, my beloved, as ye have always obeyed,
> not as in my presence only, but now much more
> in my absence, work out your own salvation with
> fear and trembling.

Your life may not look quite like your neighbor's or your pastor's or even your parents', but all of us have been given the keys to living a victorious life and overcoming the enemy. The beautiful thing about Jesus is that He is an equal-opportunity employer. The Bible says in Romans 2:11,

> For there is no respect of persons with God.

If I applied the Word of God to my life, my problem, and my situations, and I was victorious, it will work for you just the same. The Bible says in Isaiah 55:11,

> So shall my word be that goeth forth out of my mouth: it shall not return unto me void, but it shall accomplish that which I please, and it shall prosper in the thing whereto I sent it.

God has given us the beautiful gift of His Word. This is our sword in battle, our comfort when we are lonely, are light unto our path, our lighthouse in a storm. When you walk through the fire, you must hold on to it. No matter what is going on in your life, you never compromise what the Word of God is asking you to do. If you compromise on one area or skip one step, take a shortcut, or cut a corner, it may seem like a small thing until everything you built comes crashing down because of a bad foundation.

Any architect knows that the foundation is very important with anything that you build. When the blueprints are laid, it is imperative to follow the instructions for the building of the foundation. Many people go through life, and they compromise on the foundation. They get impatient or in their feelings, and they take a shortcut during the building process. Many times they don't suffer the consequences of their shortcut until years later down the road. When you try to build without the Word of God as the chief cornerstone, your life will come falling apart. When you build on the foundation of the Word of God without compromise, the storms will come, but they will not prevail against you! The foundation will stand through whatever the enemy uses to try to blow it down.

It may not come as fast as you would like, but taking the time to build your life correctly will be worth it in the end. The Bible says in Job 23:10,

> But He knoweth the way that I take; when He hath tried me, I shall come forth as gold.

God will put you through the fire to test you, to try you, to purify you and mold you into what He has for you. Just imagine you are going into surgery, and they have not given you any anesthetics. It is up to you to take those anesthetics on your own. God gave you all the medicine you need to take to make it through the surgery. It will be very painful for you if you try to go through the process without taking the medication. God is not going to force you to read His Word, get in His presence, praise Him in the storm, worship Him in the valley, or seek His face for strength. He already gave you everything you need to survive; but like a daily vitamin, it is up to you to take it.

Many people can't understand why God just doesn't force it on us. God gave us free will in order to get the glory out of our lives. If He just forced everything on you and brought you through the fire and the wilderness like a robot, He wouldn't get as much glory out of that. He gets glory when we choose to let Him be the source of our strength, our first responder in a crisis, our GPS in a lost world, and everything else we need in this life. People try to replace God with so many things in this life, but when you choose to surrender it all, take up your cross, and follow God, it shows the evidence of His power, love, and grace through our lives. It is on display for the world to see, and this is how God wins souls without forcing them.

Remember who you are living for and who is watching you when you are in the fire. Remember that you can't have a testimony without a test. Remember that you were put on this earth to give God glory. Remember that Jesus loves you no matter what you are going through. Remember that the Bible says in Romans 8:28 (full chapter):

> And we know that all things work together for
> good to them that love God, to them who are the
> called according to his purpose.

This is how you survive the fire. That is how you learn to live in the fire. Just know that the fire is a path that leads to the glory of God.

CHAPTER 12

Abducted from the Promised Land

We spent a lot of time talking about the journey through the fire toward the promise. What happens when you have made it through the wilderness and are already living in the promised land, but you mess up? What happens when you fall short after obtaining the promised land? Maybe you have been operating and living in the promise, but for some reason, you gave in to some temptation—maybe you've caved under some pressure, maybe you allowed yourself to revert to your default settings? What now?

It is very possible for God to pick you up from the promised land and put you back into the wilderness. There are many reasons for this. One of the biggest reasons God has to shake things up is because we get too comfortable in the promised land. We get spiritually fat because things are going too good. Some people only seek God when things get bad in their life. When everything starts going smooth, they put God in the back burner. God no longer becomes the center of their life. You could have prayed for marriage, ministry, or whatever your dream is to come to pass, and when it did, you stopped praying. You may have been going through the fire and asked God to deliver you, and once He did, you stopped seeking Him. If we don't have the discipline to seek God whether things are good or bad, God will keep picking us up and dropping us off in the middle of the fire or wilderness until we do better. This spiritual abduction is just a way for God to get us back on the right track in our relationship with Him. Through sacrifice, amazing things happen for us spiritually that also benefit us physically, but when we get too comfortable in the promised land, we get too lazy, or think sacrifice is not necessary anymore.

When we are going through hard times, we tend to be on our toes a little bit more spiritually. We are more alert to our spiritual surroundings. When things start going good, we can get kind of lazy—spiritually, and slowly start removing our armor. This allows the enemy to come in with a sneak attack. Many times when we fall after walking with God, we wonder, how in the world did I get so low? How in the world did I end up back here? How did I slip up in the same old tricks I used to fall in before?

The reason we end up back in Egypt after being delivered is because we let our guard down. We let people get close to us who do not have good intentions, or they give us bad counsel. We start allowing ourselves to compromise in little areas like entertainment. We start getting relaxed and not guarding our conversations. The Bible says to give no place to the devil. When we start compromising in these small areas, we allow the devil to get a foot inside the door of our minds. That is all he needs to really make a mess of things. Once he gets his foot in the door, he is going to slide his shoulder in; once he gets his shoulder in, he is going to pry the door open with his hand and snatch you up. This is what the Bible likes to call a stronghold. The devil has infiltrated the walls of your mind and abducted your heart.

You started off just being bitter because someone hurt you. You didn't give it to God, and you let the bitterness take root and start to grow. Eventually that bitterness is going to produce fruit. Let's say the reason you are bitter is because your spouse cheated on you. When you found this out, sadness, hurt, and resentment immediately hit your heart. The more you thought about it, the more bitter you started to become. That bitterness will start to suggest things to your mind once you let it take root. The bitterness will tell you, "Well, since they cheated on you, you need to make them pay." or "You might as well treat them badly, better yet, why don't you go out and cheat as well." If you entertain those thoughts that the bitterness presented, your flesh will start giving you justifications to carry out the sin. "You deserve to go out and sleep with someone else, it is not fair they got to do it and you didn't," "They don't love you if they've cheated on you," "You need to go find someone who really loves you and will show you how to treat you right."

From your wound, sin is born if not addressed. If you allow it to keep bleeding, and don't go to the spiritual emergency room and pay a visit to Doctor Jesus, you will end up a casualty on the bed of sin. This is why when you are living for God, and doing your best to do great things for the kingdom, the enemy will often use people close to you to wound you. Sometimes, it won't be people, but a situation that you are going through. The enemy knows if he can get you in your feelings, he can start suggesting things to you. This maneuver allows him to distract you. You take your eyes off the goal, the mission, the promised land and start looking for a way out of the misery you feel. Instead of pursuing Jesus, you pursue the quick shortcut out. The end result of this is always a spiritual abduction by the enemy. He lures you off the road of righteousness and takes you back to where God delivered you from, or sometimes even lower.

I live on Fort Campbell on the Kentucky side. Fort Campbell is on the state line that separates Kentucky and Tennessee. That is what it is like when you are living in the promised land. You are one step from being in the promised land or to be right back in Egypt. You are one choice, one moment, one mistake away from crossing that line and losing out on the promises of God. You look at the story of the prodigal son and how he chose to leave his father's home. He had a few choices to make, and the choices he made resulted in him leaving his father's home where he had plenty, and living among the pigs eating their leftovers. When you start living in the promised land, you will always be one choice away from giving up everything God has blessed you with, to go back to living with the pigs. The enemy will try to get you to think that he has something better for you outside the will of God, but this is where your faith needs to kick in strong. You have to trust God and know that He is your Father. You need to know in your heart that not only does He want what is best for you, He only holds what is best for you in the palm of His hand. No matter what the enemy tries to flash in front of your eyes, keep your eyes on Jesus. Never remove yourself from the promised land, by following the temptation of the enemy. The end result of following your flesh and the enemy will always be the same.

The Bible says, the enemy has come to kill, steal, and destroy. He wants to kill your dream before it ever comes to life. If he cannot kill it at birth, he wants to steal it from you after you start operating in it. If you allow him to steal it from you, it is possible for it to be destroyed depending on the choices you made.

It is so refreshing to know that even though we are not perfect, we serve a loving and merciful God. He knows that sometimes we will mess it all up. He knows that sometimes we are going to drop the ball. That is why He gave us the gift of repentance. You may mess up, but never be too proud to ask God to forgive you, and to return to your Father's home. The route may not always be pretty to get back into the promised land, but it will be worth it.

Remember you had to go through the wilderness to get to the promised land in the first place. You had to survive the attacks, the war, and the fire. If for some reason you get abducted, you may have to go through all these things again. In fact, God may allow the wilderness to be even harder and the fire to be even hotter. This is not to punish you. The Bible says in Proverbs 3:11–12 (NIV):

> My son, do not despise the LORD's discipline,
> and do not resent his rebuke, because the LORD
> disciplines those he loves, as a father the son he
> delights in.

He is not some mean God trying to smack you around and make you pay every time you mess up. He is not saying, "You know what, I hate you, and you are such a failure." He is not looking down at you with eyes burning with condemnation saying, "I am going to make this guy's life miserable." He is a gracious and wise Father. He is looking down and saying, "Because I love you so much, I must correct you in a way that you never forget." If your kids play with the socket or the hot stove, you are going to correct them in a way that they know this is serious business. You are correcting them for their own good.

If you mess up, and it seems like the one mistake you made is causing you so much trouble, don't be discouraged. The Bible says in Romans 6:23,

> For the wages of sin is death, but the gift of God
> is eternal life in Christ Jesus our Lord.

There is a death that comes when we sin. That death could be to our marriage, our ministry, or even our promise, but we serve a God who specializes in resurrection. He can bring those dead things back to life. It may seem like all hope is gone, but that is not the case with Jesus Christ. You may have to take up your cross all over again. You may have to go through the process once again and die to self, but God loves when we are in that state of brokenness. The Bible says in James 4:6 (KJV):

> But he giveth more grace. Wherefore he saith,
> God resisteth the proud, but giveth grace unto
> the humble.

God can do much more with a broken soul than He can with a proud heart. Sometimes God will allow an abduction to take place just to break you. If you look at the story when Jesus broke the bread and fed it to the disciples. It is the same concept. Jesus wants to break you in order to use you to feed the lost of this world. He may have to allow an abduction to take place to get you out of your comfort zone or teach you somethings that you couldn't be taught in your current state of mind. Just be encouraged and know that God is with you at all times. He is with you at your lowest moments even when it does not feel like it. Sin can separate us from God, but God is always one call a way. He is omnipresent. He sees it all, and He knew about it before you even came and prayed about it. No matter what situation you find yourself in, trusting in God is the key that opens every door.

CHAPTER 13

The Characteristics of Christianity

Everybody claims to be a Christian, but in the world we are living in, it does not seem that many really understand what it means to be a Christian. Are you a Christian just because you acknowledge God in a victory speech? Are you a Christian because you attend church once a week? Are you a Christian because you always remember to say grace before you eat? Are you a Christian because you don't say curse words? What qualifies me to be a Christian?

The whole point of Christianity is to follow Jesus. Jesus came down to earth and set an example through His lifestyle, His teachings, and the Word of God for us to emulate. He never promised that it would be easy, nor did He promise that it would always be fun, but He did say there is a reward for those who endure till the end.

The characteristics of your faith should be evident in the way you live your life. None of us are perfect, but our walk on this earth should reflect what is in the Word of God. The problem is many people have written their name on a sign-in sheet, but their name may not be written on the only list that matters. The Bible says in Matthew 7:21–23:

> Not every one that saith unto me, Lord, Lord, shall enter into the kingdom of heaven; but he that doeth the will of my Father which is in heaven. Many will say to me in that day, Lord,

Lord, have we not prophesied in thy name? And in thy name have cast out devils? and in thy name done many wonderful works? And then will I profess unto them, I never knew you: depart from me, ye that work iniquity.

Many people are checking off on a list that in the eyes of men qualifies them to be a follower of Christ, but yet their names are not written on the Lamb's Book of Life. There is a blueprint for the way believers should live their lives. The problem is many people never take a look at the blueprint and apply it to their life. They may glance at it casually, and not follow it, or they may look at it and reject it because they feel they have a better plan for their life.

Without sounding too deep, being a Christian means you are going to have to do a lot of things you don't feel like doing. There is a war going on between your flesh and your spirit, and each one of them is fighting for your soul. If you follow the blueprint of the scriptures, your spirit man will grow and excel, but if you give in to the desires of the flesh, your carnal man will take over, and you will be destroyed. Many times it will take faith to be obedient to what God is asking of you. Our flesh does not like to sacrifice or deal with any kind of discomfort, but the Bible demands this of us. Christianity is a beautiful thing, and it is not all doom and gloom, but it was never meant to be comfortable.

Many people fail to understand this. They want this air-conditioning Christianity. They want to be able to control the temperature. If things get too rough or too hard, they want to be able to hit the switch and adjust things to the temperature they like it. This is why many Christians never overcome situations in their life. Instead of obeying scripture and following biblical principle, they avoid dealing with issues in their life or areas that they struggle in.

Jesus calls us to love our enemies and bless those who do us wrong. Many people's flesh resists this, and they would rather get revenge, curse someone out, or just ignore the issue altogether and never speak to the individual ever again. God calls us to forgive people, but many people feel that the people who hurt them don't deserve their forgiveness. Their inability to trust that God will take care of them if they would follow the scripture, regardless of what it looks like, keeps them from ever experiencing the beauty of Christianity.

One of the greatest calls of Christianity and following Christ is to love. Many people do not even understand what love really is. They may not have experienced it, never received it, or they have a wrong concept of what it is because of things they went through early on in life. There are some who believe they love their spouse, their children, their enemy, and anyone else God has called them to love, but they are far from the truth. Love and sacrifice go hand in hand. If you don't have sacrifice, you don't have love. When you love someone, you sacrifice how you feel, what you want, what you think, your time, your money, your heart, your pride, and so much more. Someone could treat you awful, but true love says, "I am going to lay down my pride, my anger, and my desire for revenge, and forgive you." You could be giving someone all the love in the world, and they never return it, but you don't hold it against them, nor do you expect to receive any as a form of payment for what you gave. True love will correct someone who is heading down a bad path. True love will embrace someone who talks bad about you behind your back. True love will forgive someone who does not deserve it. True love will bless an enemy with their own coat when it is freezing outside. True love will take all the sin in the world on its shoulders, be beaten, humiliated, spit on, rejected, carry a cross, and be nailed to it for the world to see. True love takes a beating that it does not deserve. True love is long-suffering, kind, and gentle.

You may say I don't agree with all this. You may say that does not sound like love, that sounds more like abuse. The problem many people have is they have this false romanticized concept of love. They are not able to receive or give love effectively because they don't understand what it really is. God is love, and in order for us to be Christians, we must reflect His love in our life. You can find out what the Bible defines as love in 1 Corinthians 13:4–8 (NIV):

Love is patient, love is kind. It does not envy, it does not boast, it is not proud. It does not dishonor others, it is not self-seeking, it is not easily angered, it keeps no record of wrongs. Love does not delight in evil but rejoices with the truth. It always protects, always trusts, always hopes, always perseveres.

Love never fails. But where there are prophecies, they will cease; where there are tongues, they will be stilled; where there is knowledge, it will pass away.

One of the things that has always stood out to me the most in this verse is the fact that love keeps no record of wrongs against it. If you really love someone like God has asked you to, you have to let go of the past. You can't keep a record of all the times a person did you wrong, and continue to throw it in their face every time you have an argument. It also says that love always hopes! Just imagine being in a marriage, and it seems like the light has completely gone out. Sitting in complete darkness, as a child of God, you should still have hope. You should hope that because you love your spouse, no matter how bad things look, God can still make a way. Toward the end, it says love always trusts. How is this possible with people who lie to you over and over again?

Looking at this definition of love, it seems pretty impossible. There is no way to fulfill this kind of love on our own. It would take a supernatural experience in our life to be able to project this kind of love on our friends, family, let alone enemies. Most people who claim to be Christian do no love their family, their spouse, their enemy, or someone who hurt them like this. The second greatest commandment in the Bible is in Matthew 22: 37:

And He said to him, "'YOU SHALL LOVE THE LORD YOUR GOD WITH ALL YOUR HEART, AND WITH ALL YOUR SOUL, AND WITH ALL YOUR MIND.'

"This is the great and foremost commandment.

"The second is like it, 'YOU SHALL LOVE
YOUR NEIGHBOR AS YOURSELF.'
"On these two commandments depend the
whole Law and the Prophets."

What does that mean for you and me? Would you do anything
to hurt yourself? Would you talk down, abuse, get revenge, or cheat
yourself out of something? Jesus did not lay down any conditions
that qualify for there to be exemptions to this rule. He commands us
to love our neighbor as we love ourselves regardless of how they treat
us or what kind of person they are. Sounds almost impossible, right?
Once again I say it would take a supernatural experience in our lives
for us to be able to love like this. The Bible says in Matthew 7:12,

> So in everything, do to others what you would
> have them do to you, for this sums up the Law
> and the Prophets.

Once again you see no stipulations. The word commands us to
do for others what we would want done for us. If you were homeless,
you would want someone to feed you. If you had a broken heart, you
would want someone to comfort you. If you were lost, you would
want someone to give you direction. If you had messed up, you
would want someone to give you a second chance. If you were going
through a hard time, you would want someone to show you some
compassion. This is easy to do for our friends and family, but what
about our enemies and strangers?
The Bible says in Matthew 5:43–48:

> You have heard that it was said, "YOU SHALL LOVE
> YOUR NEIGHBOR and hate your enemy." "But I
> say to you, love your enemies and pray for those
> who persecute you, so that you may be sons of
> your Father who is in heaven; for He causes His
> sun to rise on *the* evil and *the* good, and sends
> rain on *the* righteous and *the* unrighteous.

"For if you love those who love you, what reward do you have? Do not even the tax collectors do the same?

"If you greet only your brothers, what more are you doing *than others?* Do not even the Gentiles do the same?

"Therefore you are to be perfect, as your heavenly Father is perfect."

Jesus is calling us to perfection! How is this possible? How can such messed-up, selfish, carnal, sinners be perfect? Once again I say to you, this cannot be done without a supernatural experience in our life.

The Bible says in 1 John 4:18,

There is no fear in love. But perfect love drives out fear, because fear has to do with punishment. The one who fears is not made perfect in love.

What does this mean? You can have the ability to do all the above through the power of the Spirit of God. On our own, we could never love the way that Jesus has called us to love, but through His Spirit living in us, we have a fighting chance.

The Bible says in 2 Timothy 1:7 (NKJV):

For God has not given us a spirit of fear, but of power and of love and of a sound mind.

When you put these two verses together, you begin to understand how this love is accomplished in our lives. Many times people are unable to love like this because they are selfish and feel they will get nothing in return. Sometimes they are unable to love like this because they feel the other person does not deserve their love. Other times they are not able to love like this because no one has ever shown them love like this. Some people are simply too lazy to put in the effort it requires to love like this. Fear causes people to be selfish. They worry that they will drive themselves crazy trying to love like this. They worry they will get nothing in return for their investment. When you realize that through the power of Jesus Christ, you can do all things, like the scripture says in Philippians 4:13 (NKJV):

> I can do all things through Christ[a] who strength-
> ens me.

You start to understand that God has got your back. You realize that though your enemy may do you wrong, and people may never return the love you give, God will always take care of you. This gives you the ability to love when it seems unfair. This is why the Bible says perfect love casteth out all fear! You don't fear anything when your faith is in God. You can obey the Word of God and know that no matter what, it will all work out for your good. We can see this truth in scripture.

> And we know that all things work together for
> good to those who love God, to those who are
> the called according to *His* purpose. (Romans
> 8:28, NKJV)

Many people know the first part of this verse, but fail to see the second part. I want to point out to you that it says "called according to His purpose." What does that mean for you and me? That means that when we purpose in our hearts to follow Jesus, and we choose to obey the Word of God the best we can, everything will work out for our good. We don't have to fear or worry about obeying the Word of God. When you get these scriptures deep into your heart, you understand that every time you follow the principles found in the Word of God, no matter how hard they may be, it will all work out for your good in the end. That is the greatest revelation you can have as a believer.

If you want to be a true follower of Jesus, you must know His love for yourself. It is not enough to know of it or to experience secondhand through someone else. You must know the love of God for yourself. The only way for this to happen is through an intimate and committed relationship with Jesus Christ. Remember how I kept saying in this chapter that it would take a supernatural experience to be able to follow some of these scriptures we have mentioned? Well, relationship with Jesus Christ is that supernatural experience you need. Once you have the Spirit of God living inside of you, it will be evident through the way you live your life. Your life is like a tree, and the world should be able to see the fruits of the Spirit growing from your tree if you are truly rooted in Jesus! We see this in the Word of God in Galatians 5:22–24 (NKJV):

> But the fruit of the Spirit is love, joy, peace, longsuffering, kindness, goodness, faithfulness, gentleness, self-control. Against such there is no law. And those *who are* Christ's have crucified the flesh with its passions and desires.

Many people who claim to be Christians do not have any of these fruits evident in their life. There are even a few who may seem to have some of them, but it is just an imitation. The fruits of the Spirit will not discriminate. From what we have learned in this chapter, you will see that your family, your friends, strangers, and even your enemy should all be able to eat of the fruits of the Spirit in your life. It is easier to do these things for people we like. The true test comes when we have to respond to people this way when we are not particularly fond of them.

The Bible says in Matthew 5:46,

> For if ye love them which love you, what reward have ye? Do not even the publicans the same?

Jesus did not suggest that we love people, He commanded it. Many people find this too hard to follow, and this is what separates true followers of Christ from casual fans. Jesus had many people following Him during the start of His ministry when He was performing miracle after miracle, but as the message began to get hard, many people fell away. There were not very many people following Jesus or even supporting Him openly when He was headed to the cross. Jesus said something very interesting in John 14:15 (NASB):

If you love Me, you will keep My commandments.

If you really love God, you are going to follow what His word commands you to do even when you don't feel like it or when it isn't easy. The problem today is we have so many people claiming to be Christians who do not follow biblical principle in their lives. Many people claim the title and live a lifestyle that is totally contradictory to the Word of God. Others will look at Christianity as a bag of trail mix, and they only want to pick out the M&Ms and leave the rest. Christianity is not a buffet line. You cannot go through the Word of God picking and choosing what scriptures you want to follow.

The Bible says in John 4:24,

God *is* a Spirit: and they that worship Him must worship *Him* in spirit and in truth.

Many people claim to worship in the Spirit. They go to church, and they worship with the praise team and shout amen during the preaching, but they do not apply the Word of God to their life on a daily basis. You can compare this to people who enjoy sports. Some people will tell you they like a certain team. They may watch a few games and can name a few of the players, but they are not truly dedicated. They are just a casual fan. A true follower of the team can tell you stats, name all the players, tell you who the coach is, tell you what college the players came from, tell you when the team is playing next, and what their win and loss record is. The difference between a fan and a follower is the dedication. The follower can sit down and

THROUGH THE FIRE TO BE ON FIRE

tell you a lot more about the team in a conversation than the fan can. The follower has more substance, more of a foundation.

This is why so many Christians have no joy, no peace, and no power to overcome. Casual Christians are always the first casualties. You have to go from being a fan to becoming a follower of Jesus. You need to get some substance and a firm foundation. Many casual fans of a team will switch loyalty to a winning team or when their favorite player gets traded. A true follower is going to be loyal to their team no matter what, win or lose. Your Christian walk should be the same. No matter if it seems like you are winning or losing, you are dedicated to following Jesus. You may be going through the fire, but because you have a foundation in the Word of God, you know that things will work out for your good. You can eat off the substance of your studies when things are rough. You can turn to scriptures like the one found in

Psalm 30:5 (NKJV):

> For His anger *is but for* a moment,
> His favor *is for* life;
> Weeping may endure for a night,
> But joy *comes* in the morning.

You can take joy in verses like this knowing that no matter what is going on in your life, Jesus will take care of you. Being a winner is a mind-set. Having the victory in your life is a choice. God has given us all the keys to living a blessed and victorious life. If you would follow the scripture and be faithful no matter what conditions you find yourself in, you will be blessed.

Many people think being blessed is a matter of conditions, but it really is a matter of position. Your conditions in life could be terrible. You could be going through the fire, going through a storm, or facing a situation that just seems impossible to overcome. You will always win if you remember that no matter your condition, you control your position.

Can you love in the fire? Can you be a peacemaker in the fire? Can you be long-suffering in the fire? Can you forgive when you're in the fire? This is the test of a true believer!

You can hit your knees in the middle of the fire and call out to God. You can lift your hands in the middle of the storm and worship the King of kings. You can dance in the darkness until the morning light breaks through to your situation. Understand that it is impossible to get into the presence of God and something not change. It is impossible to worship God with all your heart and not feel some joy, peace, or love once you leave His presence. This is one of the greatest revelations of learning how to live in the fire. Once you learn to trust God in the fire, you will always produce the true fruit of a Christian. You must become rooted in Jesus. When you commit yourself to walking with Jesus, everyone will be able to see the fruits of true discipleship in your life. The Bible says in Psalm 1:1–6:

> Blessed *is* the man
> Who walks not in the counsel of the ungodly,
> Nor stands in the path of sinners,
> Nor sits in the seat of the scornful;
> But his delight *is* in the law of the LORD,
> And in His law he meditates day and night.
> He shall be like a tree
> Planted by the rivers of water,
> That brings forth its fruit in its season,
> Whose leaf also shall not wither;
> And whatever he does shall prosper.
> The ungodly *are* not so,
> But *are* like the chaff which the wind drives away.
> Therefore the ungodly shall not stand in the judgment,
> Nor sinners in the congregation of the righteous.
> For the LORD knows the way of the righteous,
> But the way of the ungodly shall perish.

CHAPTER 14

Get Comfortable Being Uncomfortable

When you put meat in the fire, it cooks. When you expose metal to fire, it heats up. When you put wood in fire, it burns. When you put plastic in fire, it melts. What kind of faith do you have inside you? Do you have faith that when you are put in the fire, it begins to cook, and the aroma can be smelled by others? The more it cooks, and is seasoned with the Word of God, the more fulfilling it will be. When you are feeling empty spiritually, it will be something you can eat off in the future to sustain you. Do you have faith that absorbs the heat of the flames and gets hot when thrown in the middle of the fire? Do you have that kind of metallike faith that when the devil comes to touch you, he screams in pain because your faith is so hot! Do you have faith that catches fire in the middle of a fire? No matter how big the flames are all around you, you refuse to be consumed. Do you keep throwing more logs of the Word of God into your fire and let your fire burn bright in the midst of your circumstance? Or do you have the kind of plasticlike faith that melts away when you see the flames surrounding you? Are you able to live in the fire, not panic, and trust God? Are you able to see the flames closing in, begin to sweat, and not retreat?

Many believers make decisions during a meltdown. They panic when they see the flames surrounding them, and they feel that they must make a decision or try to fix their problem right then and there. They don't like sweating in the fire. They don't like that feeling of the unknown. People like to feel secure and in control of their life, and when this is not happening, they often panic. Many believers want to know why they are going through what they are going through. They try to figure out what they can do to stop the pain, change the uncertainty, and get some security. Other believers have a complete meltdown when they feel the heat. Their marriage may seem to be on its last leg, so they stop running. They may feel like the promotion at the job is never coming, so they quit. They may feel lonely and feel like their time is running out to be in a relationship, so they marry the first person who comes along. When they get in uncomfortable positions, they feel a desperation to get things back to a place that they are comfortable in.

What they fail to realize is that many times, these are just distractions from the enemy. If he knows he can get you to have a meltdown in the fire, he will continue to start small fires in your life to keep you distracted. Many people panic and waste all their time running from fire to fire trying to put them all out. They get overwhelmed and depressed, and eventually they have a meltdown. During this meltdown, they make choices that further destroy them or cause even more grief in their life. You have to get to the point where you understand that being in the fire is part of Christianity. You cannot escape it. The Bible says in 1 Peter 4:12–19 (KJV):

> Beloved, think it not strange concerning the fiery trial which is to try you, as though some strange thing happened unto you:
>
> But rejoice, inasmuch as ye are partakers of Christ's sufferings; that, when his glory shall be revealed, ye may be glad also with exceeding joy.
>
> If ye be reproached for the name of Christ, happy are ye; for the spirit of glory and of God

resteth upon you: on their part he is evil spoken of, but on your part he is glorified.

But let none of you suffer as a murderer, or as a thief, or as an evildoer, or as a busybody in other men's matters.

Yet if any man suffer as a Christian, let him not be ashamed; but let him glorify God on this behalf.

The fire will show you what you are made of. Many people say they believe in Jesus, but this is not good enough for God. It is not enough to say, "I believe Jesus is real, and He died for me." God wants to know that you not only believe that He is real, but that you believe He loves you and is concerned with what you are going through. He wants you to get to that point that you can keep your cool in the fire. He wants you to get to that point where you don't make rash decisions because you start sweating when you see the flames. He wants you be like the three Hebrew boys who saw the fire, but never wavered in their faith toward God. He wants to know that not only do you believe in His sacrifice, but you believe in His word. God wants to know that you trust Him with your life even when things don't look or go the way you want. This is why knowing the Word of God is so important.

Having the Word of God inside you transforms your mind. It changes the way you look at the fiery furnace, the lion's dens, or dark pits of your life. The Bible says in Romans 10:17 (KJV):

So then faith cometh by hearing, and hearing by the Word of God.

You must read the Word, and hear the Word of God on a regular basis. It is like a student who is studying for a test. You spend hours in your textbook getting familiar with the subject. You take notes and listen to the teacher and try to memorize as much about the subject as you can. Eventually all the knowledge you absorbed will be tested to see how much of it you have retained and actually know. It is the same thing with your walk with the Lord. The more Word you have in you, the greater the test will be. It is one thing to go to church, hear the preacher say, "God is a provider," and for you to shout, "Amen!" It is an entirely different thing to be in need, with your back against a wall, and trusting God to provide your needs. It is one thing to sing a song about God's healing power, and a completely different thing to get a report from the doctor and have to trust God to heal your body. Many times when the heat gets turned up in a believer's life, they complain, panic, and quit. They get depressed, and they become bitter, because they feel like what they are going through is unfair. In these moments when you are standing in the fire, the truth is revealed. If you have faith in God, you will not have a meltdown. You will be able to stand in that fire and be content. You will be able to see the flames and say, "I trust God." You will be able to say in your heart, "It may be hot in here, but I know that my God will not allow me to be consumed." The Bible says in Romans 8:28 (KJV):

> And we know that all things work together for good to them that love God, to them who are the called according to his purpose.

When you know the Word, and you really believe that God loves you, you can have faith in the fire. You can be in an uncomfortable situation and be comfortable. You will have the ability to talk to God about how you feel, but not get mad, or make rash decisions when things don't go the way you think they should go. The Bible says in Isaiah 55:8–9 (NKJV):

> "For My thoughts *are* not your thoughts,
> Nor *are* your ways My ways," says the LORD.
> "For *as* the heavens are higher than the earth,
> So are My ways higher than your ways,
> And My thoughts than your thoughts."

Sometimes you just have to sit back in the fire and say, "God, You must know something and see something that I don't." Oftentimes God uses the fire to make us better. When we go through difficult situations, it brings out the fruits of the Spirit in us. God may be trying to teach you to be more patient, more loving, more long-suffering, or many other things. You might not understand it while you are in the fire, but once you come out on the other side into your blessing, you will see why God allowed you to go through those flames. You will see all the things that God burned away from you in the fire. Paul understood this very well. He knew that being blessed was not a matter of his conditions, but a matter of his position. His conditions were not always the best, but he did not change on his position toward God. He continued to worship, be faithful, and dedicated to his relationship and ministry. He wrote in Philippians 4:10–13 (NIV):

> I rejoiced greatly in the Lord that at last you renewed your concern for me. Indeed, you were concerned, but you had no opportunity to show it. I am not saying this because I am in need, for I have learned to be content whatever the circumstances. I know what it is to be in need, and I know what it is to have plenty. I have learned the secret of being content in any and every situation, whether well fed or hungry, whether living in plenty or in want. I can do all this through him who gives me strength.

Paul had complete faith in God. His faith did not waver when things were uncertain. Paul sat in jail many times not knowing what the future would hold for him. He knew his future was uncertain, but he was certain no matter what, God would do what was best for him.

Do you have the ability to keep your cool in the fire? Pain is really a sign of promotion with God. Your ability to manage pain, conflict, and adversity will determine how much God can bless you with. The bigger the blessing you get from God, the bigger the attack will be from the enemy to steal it. This is why God will allow you to be tested over and over again. He is trying to make you strong for what He has prepared for you. The enemy is not going to just sit back and let you be blessed, let you be used, and let you be on fire for God. He will do anything he can to destroy what God has started in you. Thankfully we know the Bible says in Philippians 1:6 (NIV):

> Being confident of this, that he who began a good
> work in you will carry it on to completion until
> the day of Christ Jesus.

The devil cannot steal, destroy, or hinder what God is doing in your life. He can test you and turn up the heat around you and try to distract you, but he cannot stop the blessings of God in your life. He couldn't force Eve to eat the apple, he could only try to trick her. He got her to take her eyes off the paradise she was in and tricked her out of her blessing. God will allow the enemy to set these fires in your life just to see how you respond. Many people waste time getting mad at people, getting depressed, and running around trying to put out all these fires on their own. They end up taking their eyes off their dream, their mission, their calling, and our God. You cannot let the small fires in your life distract you from what God is trying to do in your life. Once you realize that your battle is not against people, you will save yourself so much time. The Bible says in Ephesians 6:12 (ESV):

> For we do not wrestle against flesh and blood, but
> against the rulers, against the authorities, against
> the cosmic powers over this present darkness,
> against the spiritual forces of evil in the heavenly
> places.

The enemy is going to use whoever he can to bring you down. Unfortunately, many times this will be the people closest

to you. **You have to realize that none of us are perfect, and we are all susceptible to an attack from the enemy. You may feel like everybody is against you, but let God deal with it. The Bible says in** Psalm 118:6 (NIV):

> The LORD is with me; I will not be afraid.
> What can mere mortals do to me?

There is nothing that can happen to you that has not already passed through the hands of God. Remember God and Satan had a conversation about Job, and Job was nowhere to be found. The battle was never Job's; it was between God and Satan. God allowed Satan to touch Job in order to prove a point to the devil. Stop wasting your time worrying about who hurt you, who did you wrong, who let you down, and keep your eyes on the one who sticks closer than a brother!

I have some wonderful news for you today! You can get comfortable in your uncomfortable situation. You don't have to throw another punch or brainstorm another hour. The Bible says in 2 Chronicles 20:15,

> And he said, Hearken ye, all Judah, and ye inhab-
> itants of Jerusalem, and thou king Jehoshaphat,
> Thus saith the LORD unto you, Be not afraid nor
> dismayed by reason of this great multitude; for
> the battle is not yours, but God's.

You don't have to panic anymore. You don't have to stress about what seems to be a bad thing that is happening in your life. You have a God on your side who is bigger than anything you face. If you don't remember anything else, remember that He loves you. He may be allowing you to face certain situations in order to make you better.

Many people assume they did something wrong when hell starts breaking loose in their life. They beat themselves down with condemnation and assume God is punishing them for not being perfect or for messing up in some area of their life. This is not always the case. Yes, sometimes God may be giving you correction, but His correction will always work out for your good. He does not punish you to make you miserable. He will punish you to make you better. Remember even if He does punish you for something you did, His love and mercy for you is so awesome, because He already paid the price for all your sins. He will never make you pay the full price for your sins, and mistakes, because He already paid for it all on the cross!

You don't have to feel sad every time you are going through hard times in life. Just remember this Bible verse in Job 23:10,

> But he knoweth the way that I take: *when* he hath
> tried me, I shall come forth as gold.

You will save yourself so much grief when you understand that walking through the fire is part of Christianity. You might as well get used to the enemy attacking you. You might as well get used to living for Jesus not always being a walk on the beach. Jesus said take up your cross, not your vacation packet. It may not be a pretty process, but the end results will always be beautiful. The enemy will try to convince you that it is not worth it, but trust God. God has blessings for you that you never ever could imagine!

No matter how uncomfortable your situation is, you can know that God is working things out for your good. If you endure the fire and trust God, you are going to come forth as pure gold! Your pain is not in vain. Your test is going to give you a testimony. Embrace the fire and learn to live in it. Learn to trust God no matter how got it gets in there. Wipe the sweat from your eyes and lift up your hands and say, "Lord, I trust You." It is okay to tell God you don't like what you are going though. It is okay to share with him how you feel about the things going on in your life. But never let your conditions dictate the position of your heart toward God. Make up in your mind to get comfortable being uncomfortable.

CHAPTER 15

The Island of Isolation

There are some seasons in your life where you simply must walk alone. The more you try to fight for someone to depend on, the longer you will be in that season. Christians really have a serious problem with insulting God. We claim to believe He is everything we need, but when we don't have someone supporting us, telling us what we want to hear, or being a shoulder for us to lean on, we love to say we are alone. We love to feel sorry for ourselves and throw a pity party. We have this mind-set that we are happy when people are doing and saying what we want, and when they are not, we get disappointed and forget that we have Jesus on our side. God becomes an afterthought instead of being the first thought. Some believers want to call Him after they called everyone else, and no one picked up or said anything encouraging to them. They want to spend some time in the presence of God after they have spent time with everything else but God. Many believers pray, worship, or read their Bible out of conviction and not out of love. They give God drive by worship. Let me pray real quickly before I got to bed. Let me read a chapter so I can say I read my Bible today. Let me play a worship song in the car so I can say I spent some time in God's presence. This is not relationship, this is religion. The Pharisees did many things in the Bible as a ritual or to be seen, but it was not in their hearts to serve and love God. Jesus knew the importance of getting alone in prayer in secret. Sometimes it just has to be you and God! Many prophets including

Jesus often found solitude to find God in a deeper intimate way, in order to get a more direct message or direction.

> Very early in the morning, while it was still dark, Jesus got up, left the house and went off to a solitary place, where he prayed. (Mark 1:35)

Jesus often withdrew to lonely places and prayed. (Luke 5:16)

> Now Moses used to take a tent and pitch it outside the camp some distance away, calling it the "tent of meeting"... The LORD would speak to Moses face to face, as a man speaks with his friend. Then Moses would return to the camp, but his young aide Joshua son of Nun did not leave the tent. (Exodus 33:7, 11)

> [Elijah] went into a cave and spent the night. And the word of the LORD came to him... a gentle whisper. (1 Kings 19:9, 12)

Many times God will allow us to be in a place of solitude and take us out of our comfort zone. It may not feel good, but this is the only way we can grow. God will allow you to be shipwrecked on life on an island all by yourself. It is easy to get negative about the shipwreck and the lack of support you have on the island. It is easy to walk up and down the shore and not see another living being in sight and allow that hopeless feeling to overwhelm you. It is easy to slip into depression because the only thing on this island is you and your wreckage.

God will allow this in your life for a season. It will be just you and your mess, your mistakes, your problems, your test, and whatever else it is going on in your life. I want to challenge you to look at it from a new perspective today. It may seem like a bad and lonely thing sitting on your island of isolation, but that is not the case. Your island of isolation is really a beautiful honeymoon resort for just you and Jesus to get intimate. He whisked you away from everybody else, just so He could have you all to Himself. He removed all your crutches just so you could learn to walk on His power alone. You got so used to calling your friends every time you had a problem. You got used to your pastor always giving you the on-time word for you to make it through your week. You got used to your money always being good, your spouse always acting right, and always having some support. God will remove you just so you can realize He is the source of your strength. He will remove those people just so you can realize nobody can love you and comfort you like He can.

Instead of being depressed on your island, run into the arms of your lover Jesus and let Him blow your mind! You cannot take a long walk in the presence of God and something not change in your spirit, your mind, and your perspective. Don't be miserable because it seems nobody supports you or is there for you. Remember you have a God who is fighting for you. You have a God who is in control of every situation in your life. You have a God who said He would never leave your or forsake you.

Sometimes we get so busy with life we make God an afterthought. God wants to be your first thought, your first desire, and your first responder. The Bible is clear that God is a jealous God. He does not put you on the island as punishment, but just to show you to lean on Him and to refocus on your relationship. You say you don't have time for Him, so He clears your schedule! Don't be upset about it. Don't sleep away the hours day after day. Use your time to get closer to God than ever before. Use your time to pray, study, and worship God like you never have before. You can never go wrong with spending time with God. There are so many benefits to being in His presence. You will realize that you wasted so much time on other people who couldn't give you the strength that God can. You will realize you wasted so much time waiting on a word from God through your pastor that you could have just gotten yourself falling at the feet of Jesus. You will realize that you wasted so much time looking for somebody to be there, that you forgot about the one who never left and was there from the start.

When you get your focus back while on the island, you will eventually see a plane land or a ship dock on the shore. God will line up everything in your life once you get your focus right. He will bring in your supporting cast to the island, and you will not be alone anymore. It may be a spouse, a best friend, a pastor, or whatever else you need. Your new perspective will show you that you survived the island without them. You only need God to make it through hard times, but He will put people in your life to just make it a little easier and to complement what He is already doing in your life. Once you understand that nobody can fix your problems or complete you like Jesus can, God will take you out of isolation and give you the desires of your heart.

Remember, God does not hate you. He is not punishing you to be mean. The Bible says those whom He loves, He corrects. He put you on the island for your own good! It is up to you how much time you spend on it and what you do with the time you have there!

Find rest, O my soul, in God alone. (Psalm 62:5)

CHAPTER 16

Spiritual Firefighters

Firefighters spend lots of time training and doing drills to practice fighting fires together, before they actually run into a building and fight a real fire. They have to be able to trust one other to watch each other's back, and do their part. Everybody has a specific task to do when inside of a burning building. There are some guys on the ground giving directions; there are other guys opening up windows, doors, and roofs to create ventilation; there are guys who are setting up ladders to enter top floors and rescue people out of the fire; and then there are the guys actually putting out the fire. Everybody has to be alert and very aware of their surroundings. If one guy is day-dreaming, or not following his proper training procedures, it could cost the life of one of his fellow firefighters. Whatever role God gives you, you need to do it without complaining. It might not be the role you wanted, but you can't lose focus being jealous over somebody else's role or complaining about the job you have.

The Bible says in Colossians 3:23,

> Work willingly at whatever you do, as though you were working for the Lord rather than for people.

You can't survive the fires of life with just anybody. Some people will actually cause more damage than good. You have people who will not follow the proper procedures, who will put you in harm's way with bad advice and choices. It is not a good feeling for you to be pulling your weight, and someone else destroys it all. You have people who are selfish, who won't help you if the fire traps you in a corner or if the ground gives way under you. They are only concerned with saving themselves, and they will leave you to burn. Then you have those who will actually pour gasoline on the fire. These people tend to accuse you and blame you for why you are going through what you are going through. You already feel uncomfortable in the heat, and they make it their mission to make you feel even more miserable about the situation. They will pour accusations on you and make you feel condemnation, regret, remorse, and just heavy in your spirit. Instead of fighting the fire with confidence and the power of the Holy Spirit, you find yourself just dragging through the house watching the flames and having an attitude of defeat and spiritual suicide.

You have to be extremely careful who you allow into your life. Some people just cannot handle where God is trying to take you. This can be anything from parents to spouses, coworkers, and friends. People have their own baggage they must handle. Sometimes you can team up and carry the load, other times what they have and what you have is just not a good fit. If you struggle with lust, you don't want to be around people who entertain and give in to lust all the time. They will not be able to help you fight that fire in your life when it arises. They will only make things worse. If you have trouble with gossiping, you can't be around people who love to talk about other people or put other people down all the time. They will not be able to help you put out that fire in your life.

You have to watch and be aware of what kinds of people you make connections with in your life. Sexual relationships are one of the biggest ways people damage themselves. People carry all kinds of spirits they are battling with. You may be struggling trying to put out the fire of rage or anger in your life. It does you no good to sleep with somebody who struggles with a spirit of lust or depression. You create soul ties when you have sexual relationships with people. God never created sex to be for multiple partners. Sex was created for a man and a wife to come together and become one flesh! This is why you must use wisdom and seek God about your relationships, and do things the way God designed. You have to protect your temple! There are other connections that we can make with people that are not sexual but just as damaging to us. You may have a friend you have known your whole life, and you really love them like a brother or sister. You may want to include them in your dreams and all the things you have planned with your life. But just because you love them does not mean they can be involved in what God is trying to do in your life. They may become a hindrance to what God is trying to do in your life. God is going to take you through the fire to test you. If you bring people who can't handle the heat, they may discourage you and convince you to turn back. When you look at the children of Israel and their report on the Promised Land, only Joshua and Caleb came back with a faith report! You want someone who will endure the fire with you and reinforce what God is trying to do in your life. You want someone who will see the flames, feel the heat, see you sweating, and say, "Hey, we can do this in Jesus's name."

If you get with the wrong people, they will always shoot down your dream or crack under pressure. You don't want to build a foundation with weak people. You don't want to start building your dream with people who are lazy, uncommitted, have no work ethic, or are full of envy. The Bible says in Luke 6:12–16:

> It was at this time that He went off to the mountain to pray, and He spent the whole night in prayer to God. And when day came, He called His disciples to Him and chose twelve of them, whom He also named as apostles: Simon, whom He also named Peter, and Andrew his brother; and James and John; and Philip and Bartholomew; and Matthew and Thomas; James the son of Alphaeus, and Simon who was called the Zealot; Judas the son of James, and Judas Iscariot, who became a traitor.

Jesus spent all night praying before He went out and chose His disciples. This shows how serious it is when you build your team. Jesus prayed all night for guidance and wisdom. His choosing of Judas also shows He prayed for the Lord's will to be done in His life. If you want to do big things for God, and survive the fires that come with walking in that direction, you need to be careful who you choose to walk with. You must pray and ask God to not only send you people who will support you, but send you people who will help you accomplish God's will for your life.

Here are some Bible verses that support this. Everybody cannot go where God wants to take you.

> Whoever walks with the wise becomes wise, but the companion of fools will suffer harm. (Proverbs 13:20)

> But now I am writing to you not to associate with anyone who bears the name of brother if he is guilty of sexual immorality or greed, or is an idolater, reviler, drunkard, or swindler—not even to eat with such a one. (1 Corinthians 5:11)

> Make no friendship with a man given to anger, nor go with a wrathful man, lest you learn his ways and entangle yourself in a snare. (Proverbs 22:24–25)

Now obviously none of us are perfect, but the fact is we must guard what God has given us. We can't compromise in order to socialize. Many people get so caught up in having friends and being accepted that they lose focus. If you focus on Jesus first, He will supply everything you need in this life. He has the perfect spouse, friend, mentor, pastor, church, job, and whatever else it is you need in this life. Don't get distracted putting all your focus into building a supporting cast or team. Put your focus into your relationship with Jesus and trust that He will order your steps. The Bible says,

> But seek ye first the kingdom of God, and his righteousness; and all these things shall be added unto you. (Matthew 6:33, KJV)

If you just focus on Jesus, everything else will come into perspective. If you focus on relationships, and marriage, and take God out of directing your decisions, you will be consumed when it is time to walk through the fire with these people. You want a team that is fireproof. You want a team that won't give in to the pressure of the heat and panic, retreat, or quit. The fact is you are incapable of putting this kind of team together without the guidance of God. You cannot see into a person's heart, only God can. They may seem to be everything you need or want, but God can see beyond the outward appearance into their heart. On the other hand, you may overlook someone because you don't think that much of them.

Joseph was thrown in jail. Many people in jail would keep running to the prison warden or prison guard in hopes of getting what they need. They would assume that these people have the power to get them to where they want to be. If Joseph had ignored those guys who came to him with their dreams, Joseph would have never gone from the prison to the palace. Don't try to push past everybody you think is insignificant in order to get to the guy who looks like they got all the power to help you. The person you need could be the person you overlook. This is why you must ask God for guidance in every step you make. Trust God to help you surround yourself with the kind of team that will help you survive the fire and not be destroyed!

CHAPTER 17

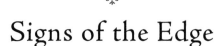

Signs of the Edge

How do you know you are on the edge of the promised land? How do you know that you are closer than you've ever been before? One of the best ways to realize you are on the edge of a new season is dramatic change that seems to be a bad thing. There could be changes in your job, you relationship, your income, your family, your location, and anything else. People don't like change—it is uncomfortable. People do not like it when something has been consistent in their life, and now it is gone. This is why it is so important to walk by faith and not by sight.

Sometimes, God has to remove some things out of your life in order to get you to the next level. Imagine yourself going to the airport, and you have got all these bags with you. When you get to the checkout counter, the attendant tells you some of these bags cannot go on board with you. In order for you to fly, you have to check, pay extra, or leave some of those bags behind. Every person's situation is different. In order for you to fly, God may be asking you to leave some people behind. In order for you to fly, God may ask you to pay a higher price to get to that final destination. In order for you to fly, God may ask you to check in your bag and pick it up later. Maybe, you have to let go of some people for a season and pick them up later.

Sometimes, life will be like an elevator when you walk with God. Everybody cannot go where God is trying to take you. Everybody is not on the same level as you. In order for you to keep going up, some people are going to have to get off on different levels. When you fight to hold on to these people or things, you keep yourself grounded from being able to take off and fly. The change in your life may not feel good, but sometimes it is absolutely necessary.

God fed the children of Israel for forty years with manna from heaven. When power was transiting from Moses to Joshua, the manna from heaven stopped. Many Israelites probably complained, and didn't understand why all of a sudden now, they had to make their own food. They did not like this change in programming. What they failed to realize was God was about to take them out of the wilderness into the Promised Land. The manna stopping was a sign that they were on the edge of something amazing.

Do not be discouraged when things stop working the way they have always worked in your life. Do not be discouraged when people let you down or drop the ball in your life. God is allowing those things to stop or change so He can take you into a new dimension. You are experiencing the signs of the edge. It might not feel like it, but you are right on the edge of something great. You are right on the edge of leaving the wilderness and entering into the promised land that God has ordained for your life. The Bible says, the work God started in you—He will see it through till its completion. God has a plan for your life since before you were born. Don't be discouraged when things are not going the way you want them to go or the way you had your blueprints laid out. God has much bigger, better blueprints for your life than you could ever imagine.

When you try to stick to your blueprints, you put God in a box. It is time to let God out of the box in your life and let Him lead you. It is uncomfortable climbing out of your box of security, but have faith! Inside your little box, you may think you have the perfect world, the perfect plans, and the perfect setup for the way you want your life to go. When all those plans and ideas start falling apart, don't be discouraged. These are just signs from God that you are on the edge. He wants you to let go of your plans and take His hand and follow Him. The waves may be crashing around in your life, and it is not a sign that you are going to sink and be destroyed, it is a sign for you to do something different to change course. It is time for you to break the pattern and go beyond the limits of your mind and operate in faith into the unknown. It is time for you to do like Peter and step off the boat and walk on water!

It takes serious faith to leave the comfort zone of the boat and walk out on to the edge and step into the water. It may look intimidating, but that is why faith is so important. If you do not have faith in God, you will never walk across the waters it takes to get you to where Jesus is. You may stand on the edge, and see the waves of change in your life. You may hear whispers from your past in the strong winds. You may see people sitting back on the boat unwilling to go with you or support your move. You cannot let any of that stop you from crossing over the edge into the water.

You cannot let people, your past, your insecurities, the enemy, or anything else stop you from crossing over the edge, the wilderness, the boat, and into the promised land. Nothing can stop you, only you, when God is with you. The Bible says, if God is for you, who can be against you? Today is your day and your moment to start walking in faith. Do not be scared of the edge or the wilderness or the waves that are rocking your boat. God is with you. He will be with you every step of the way, if you acknowledge Him in every step you take.

Many people in this life give up when they get to the edge. They don't like the changes they see. They don't like the people that are jumping ship. They don't like not knowing every point in the plan from point A to Z. They don't like walking out on faith, knowing there is a risk that they could sink. They don't like the pressure they feel from the enemy, haters, and naysayers who want them to stop. They don't like the hours of sleep they must sacrifice to sow into their dream, fight back the darkness with praise, and study the Word to build their faith. They don't like the sacrifice, like Abraham and his son. They don't like the idea of what it will take to climb that mountain and what it will cost them at the top. They don't like the idea of walking through the wilderness alone. They want support, comfort, and someone who is cheering them on. They don't like when people talk about them because they are doing something outside of the box, so they climb back in their shell. They give up because nobody in their family or immediate circle has ever accomplished what they have set their focus on to accomplish. They give up on the promise, and the promised land, and settle for less than what God intended them to have. They look at the cost, and they say it is too high.

What are you going to do? They give up because they are walking by sight and leaning on their own understanding. This is causing restrictions in their life. The Bible says, He whom the Son has set free, is free indeed. You are free to dream. You are free to overcome. You are free to be all the things God is calling you to be. You are free to live free from abuse. You are free to break the generational curses in your life. You are free to walk toward the promised land. You are free to achieve every dream that has been birthed inside you.

You have the dream, and you have a choice. Everything that is worth something in this life costs something. Everything that is worth something will not come easy. God won't let it come easy, because He wants it to be a God thing. He wants you to have a testimony for His glory. He wants to be the center point of your success. He wants you and the world to know you've made it where you are by the grace and power of the Almighty God. The revelation of the truth that He is real can be exhibited through the ups and downs and testimony of your life! Do not be discouraged when things are not going easy in life. God is preparing you for His greatness. What a privilege and honor to be chosen by the Creator of this universe. God wants to use you and everything about your life to be an exhibition of His power. Your setback is really just a setup for God to do something amazing. There is no telling how far you could go in life, if you let God be the center of it. There is no telling how high you could fly, if you would just surrender the controls into His hands. Life may have not given you a fair shake. Things may have been rough, but all these things that seemed like deficiencies and handicaps can be used in a mighty way for the glory of God!

Today is your day. You may be looking ahead of you, and you see nothing but obstacles, opposition, and discouragement. You may look behind you and see an ugly past and a trail of tears, heartache, letdowns, and betrayal. You may look to your left and right and realize you are going to have to go through this alone with God. But I want you to be encouraged no matter what is behind you, or in front of you, and know that God is inside you. If there is a Goliath in front of you, that means there is a David inside you. If there is mess behind you, there is a message in front of you. If there is a test before you, there will be a testimony afterward. Press toward Jesus, and never doubt your faith in God! You have to go through the fire to be on fire.

CONCLUSION

After the Fire

When I started writing this book, I let you guys know about the trials I was currently facing. That was six months ago since I wrote that first chapter. I have had many ups and downs as I fought for my marriage and waited for what would happen on my job. While fighting for my marriage through fasting, praying, and just seeking God for direction, God humbled me and showed me a new way to see my marriage. Through the process, I started writing a book on marriage. God not only revived, renewed, and restored my marriage, but also showed me the blueprint in His word to help others who want to get married or who feel like their marriage is on the brink of ending. I can tell you today my marriage is wonderful, and I am so in love with my wife. God had to show me how to handle things in a different way and allow Him to fight my battles for me. He showed me to have faith in Him and to cast my cares upon Him and watch Him work and make the changes.

As far as my job, I ended up getting demoted one rank. I didn't think it was fair, but I knew God was in control. I have had to eat a big piece of humble pie walking around my job and everyone seeing me demoted, but the way I carry myself has helped me to inspire, encourage, and win even more people for Christ. I was worried about my finances taking a hit, but God has provided for my family every step of the way. Like He literally blessed us with money out of thin air. Somehow I have survived these six months, and I am getting ready to go back to the board and get my rank back. God literally made a way out of no way! It has not been easy, and every day has not felt so good, but God has kept me and used me. Watching God provide and take care of me gives me passion and boldness, but going through the fire and enduring the wounds gives me compassion and humbleness.

There is a reason God puts us through the fire. Every time I come out on the other side, I feel stronger in my faith in the Lord. It seems that I get a season of rest and relaxation, and then God sends me through another fire that is hotter than the last. The more I walk with God, the less I panic in the face of adversity. People often say God gives His toughest battles to His strongest soldiers, but I believe God creates His toughest soldiers through the hardest battles. If you are able to endure the fire, God will use you to help someone else through it. The fire will try your faith and give you boldness. The fire will try your heart and expose what is inside it. The fire will bring out the best and the worst in you, and it is up to you which one you walk out of it with in your hand, and which you leave behind you to burn. The fire will give you compassion for people, help you to slow down, be patient and more understanding when other people are afflicted. The fire will keep you humble and remind you that you can only make it by the grace of God. Trust the process, and do not be discouraged. There is a reason you are in the fire. Learn to live in it, learn to excel in it, learn to grow in it, and most of all, remember that God is always with you in it.

ABOUT THE AUTHOR

I grew up in Chicago Illinois with my mother, sister, and two brothers. We lived in a shelter for a year before my mother got her own apartment. Do to the constant violence at my school, my mother chose to homeschool me from the 5th grade until I went to college.

I worked full time since the age of 11 for my landlord. I did minor maintenance, construction, and cleaning of all his apartment complexes in Chicago. At the age of 18 I joined the US Army. One year after my training I was deployed to Bagdad, Iraq where I served 12 months on Force Protection. I came back to the states for about a year and a half before I was deployed again to Kandahar Afghanistan for another 12 months. Do to the constant deploying and my backslidden lifestyle I ended up getting a divorce. I later remarried a childhood friend and shortly after for deployed to South Korea. During this period of my life God really started dealing with me, and revealing His purpose for my life. I went through many trials, heartbreaks, letdowns and storms, but God was faithful through it all. God gave me a new perspective on why certain things had to happen in my life, and though those many lessons and trials my motto was born, Through the fire to be on fire. This book was birthed from the fires I have endured, and I hope it will bring you through the ones you face as well.

CPSIA information can be obtained
at www.ICGtesting.com
Printed in the USA
LVHW032327171118
597482LV00001B/57/P

9 781640 796874